*borderline
culture*

borderline culture

The
Politics
of
Identity
in
Four
Twentieth-
Century
Slavic
Novels

Tomislav Z. Longinović

the university of arkansas press   fayetteville 1993

This book was designed by Chiquita Babb using the Garamond and Stempel Garamond typefaces.

The paper used in this publication meets the minimum requirements of the American National Standard for Permanence of Paper for Printed Library Materials z39.48-1984. ∞

Library of Congress Cataloging-in-Publication Data

Longinović, Toma, 1955–
    Borderline culture : the politics of identity in four twentieth
-century Slavic novels / Tomislav Z. Longinović.
        p.   cm.
    Includes bibliographical references (p.   ) and index.
    ISBN 1-55728-262-5 (c)
    1. Slavic literature—20th century—History and criticism.
I. Title.
PG507.L66   1993
891.8—dc20   92–20696
                                                        CIP

For my daughters, Una and Nina,
to remember those lands-in-between where their parents came from

In the beginning, there was no earth and no people. Everywhere was water. There were only the Lord and the devil, who at that time lived together.

Ancient Bulgarian Apocryphal Genesis

Dread is of life as a whole—that is, of death as end, ground, and the border of life.

Martin Heidegger, *Being and Time*

Contents

Preface

This study of Slavic literature and culture was initiated in 1986, years before the collapse of the Soviet Union, Yugoslavia, and Czechoslovakia was in sight. The rapid change in the historical and political contexts in this part of the world made the task of the literary scholar and cultural historian confronting these works particularly difficult, due to the lingering sense that the unfolding of history inevitably outdoes any particular effort to grasp it and in so doing inevitably petrifies it. Nevertheless, the influence of political institutions and cultural formations on the articulations of individual identity in the works of Mikhail Bulgakov, Witold Gombrowicz, Danilo Kiš, and Milan Kundera still has a relevance that reaches beyond the apparently bygone era of totalitarianism. The damage done both to the individual and collective identity of the Slavic peoples after decades of political oppression is evident in the violent nationalist resurgence in the region.

I have confronted here some of the questions pertinent to the area of comparative Slavic studies that have haunted me both as a scholar and as a writer from the moment I have immersed myself in the fascinating world of literature and culture from this part of the world: Is it possible to use such a homogeneous historical, cultural, and literary category that the term "Slavic" suggests? Are there still some common cultural elements that can be recognized, traced, and recuperated from common Slavic origins? If these common elements exist, how are they retained, transformed, or lost within the particular national culture after the Slavic migrations to the East, the West, and the South? What is the role of Christianity and its schisms in the process of cultural differentiation of Slavic nations? What is the impact of Western ideas of Enlightenment and romanticism on the formation of Slavic modern, national cultures? How are Marxist ideas refracted through the prism of Russian culture and that of other Slavic countries to which the socialist revolution has been exported from Russia? And, finally, what is the place of those writers in the twentieth century who oppose realism and embrace the borderline cultural position in the historical evolution of Slavic literatures? The detailed answers to these questions would certainly require several volumes. Therefore, this study, and especially its introductory part, is limited to the perspective and scope of a prolegomenon, a general postulation of the problematics that calls for further revisions and additions in future contributions to the field of comparative Slavic studies.

One problem with the concept of "Slavdom" at the end of the twentieth century stems from the fact that it has definite echoes of the nineteenth-century Russian-inspired Panslavic movement. My intention is to preserve the concept of Slavic culture both from the inclusive usage preferred by some Russians (namely, that everything Slavic is actually Russian) and from the exclusion and downplaying of the common cultural origin by some Catholic Slavs. Rather than postulating Slavic cultural identity as a monolithic and unchangeable concept, I intend to show its problematic, borderline nature by studying four twentieth-century writers who wrote in Russian, Polish, Serbo-Croatian, and Czech. Because Slavs were forced to exist between Asia and Europe by geographic, historical, and political circumstances, they have developed a cultural identity marked by dualism and impermanence that is perhaps most apparent in the destruction of monuments that follows every historical overturn (Christians destroy pagan temples, Communists destroy churches, nationalists destroy Lenin's statues, etc.). Current territorial disputes between ethnic factions in the former Soviet Union and in Yugoslavia emphasize the importance of establishing new borders, yet prove that the violence and human tragedy required by the task make the struggle over borders superfluous and absurd. However, since the borders have been changed so much more often in this part of the world than in Europe proper, the resulting cultural practices in Russia and East-Central Europe have been marked by the sense of a loss of proper identity that often results in horrible compensatory manifestations of the totalitarian wish to control and to impose identity at any price.

Finally, I need to say that my analysis of Slavic literature and culture uses psychoanalytic terminology that is adapted to characterize the political mechanisms of power as they influence both the individual and the collective processes of identity formation. This method, which will later be defined as psychopolitics, rests on a hypothesis that identity and culture can be accounted for in psychoanalytic terms only if the broader political context is taken into account. This does not simply mean that literature reflects the political climate, but that literature is an intersection of discourses latent in a given culture and made manifest by an individual author. The writers I have selected for this study have tried consciously to detach themselves from politics, which makes the analysis of their works doubly interesting. First, their rejection of political reality forces them to construct a literary universe that is highly idiosyncratic; second, that rejection reveals some of the most crucial aspects of the "political unconscious" in Slavic cultures.

In closing, I would like to thank all my friends, colleagues, and family members who have supported me during the years that went into writing and preparing this book.

The chapter on Kundera appeared in a slightly different form in *Milan Kundera and the Art of Fiction: Critical Essays* (New York: Garland Publishing, Inc.), 1992.

borderline
culture

Introduction:

Origins
of
Borderline
Poetics
in
Slavic
Culture

Slavic literatures clearly show that writing and literature do not develop in a social vacuum or in an elevated aesthetic sphere that is beyond the reach of the mundane practices of politics and ideology. Even the oldest ideologemes, mythological accounts, and religious records point to the fact that politics and literature became opposed and separated in the moment of semiotic collision between the written word of Christianity and the oral tradition of Slavic tribes. Writing is a technique that codifies by recording what is perceived as a permanent trace of the word of those who are literate. Given this kind of political advantage, the hegemonic forces (Christian scribes and the supporting feudal order) actively displaced the formulas of the Slavic oral tradition outside the literate zone, transforming the oral tradition into nonculture. The tribal social order was transformed by Christian culture, which established urban centers for the dissemination of literacy for the ruling classes. On the other hand, Slavic peasantry kept alive ancient pagan beliefs and practices, which were excluded from written culture. The Slavic peasants were forced into resistance by the very fact of their illiteracy.[1]

Writing, as the new technological device for the recording of sanctioned truth, was introduced through Christian institutions into the Slavic world—in Old Church Slavic for the tribes in the cultural domain of Byzantium (e.g., Bulgarians, Serbs, Macedonians, Russians) and in Latin for the tribes that were converted and dominated by Rome (e.g., Poles, Czechs, Slovaks, Slovenes, Croats).[2] Writing arrived to the Slavic world as a sign of a new single god, a sign replacing the polytheistic multitude that had been celebrated through the spoken word (the oral tradition) and ornamental artifacts with their strong ritual function. Therefore, the institutional status of writing became inextricably tied to Christianity and ways in which it assimilated ritual practices and meanings present in ancient Slavic mythemes. Writing was introduced into the field of the dominantly oral culture as a new ideological force employed to suppress the old world of pagan worship. This repression by the signifier created a gap within the polysemic world of gods, demons, and spirits, which were supposed to be subsumed under One Holy Signifier introduced by the clergy. Supported by the image of Christ, ecclesiastical writing was a transparent expression of the word of God, a silent word that expelled the oral semiotic production into a zone of nonculture, codifying it as demonic and subversive. Slavic popular culture was therefore preserved as a practice exterior to writing, but as a practice that will always be already interior to it. The colonial authority of writing in Slavic culture is subverted as it is permeated by low, excluded discourses.

This marginal position of popular culture, at first perceived as nonculture by the hegemonic forces, was transformed with the spread of literacy into the so-called "secular culture," a characteristic of the transition from the medieval to the modern cultural formations. With the occurrence of socialist revolutions in the twentieth century, this marginal position became occupied by the writer, who was labeled as the dissident by the totalitarian political forces and often imprisoned, exiled, or liquidated. This originary rift between writing and speech provides a new perspective for the area of comparative Slavic studies. The identification of congruent or similar semiotic units between different Slavic cultures, sought by Jakobson, Lotman, and other paralinguists, does not provide an entirely adequate frame for understanding this liminal quality of Slavic cultural identity. Paradoxically, what unites Slavic cultures is exactly the fact of the primal psychopolitical repression instituted by Christianity. The development of literary institutions is set in motion after this semiotic colonization, initiated by the collision of different political, historical, and cultural formations, which results in the subsuming and supressing of oral culture by Christian writing. This semiotics of difference, devoted to the study of political regulation of signifying systems, is what I propose to call psychopolitics.[3]

The struggle for the hegemony over the writing practice and the resulting codification of meaning was inevitably guided by the sharp opposition between "high" and "low" cultural values, between the "divine" and the "demonic," between "revolutionary" and "reactionary" modes of writing. The medieval control of writing by Christian clergy was possible because it was supported by strict feudal division between lords and serfs. Literacy became a privilege of the ruling classes, while illiterate peasants continued to preserve archaic cultural elements. The class difference was congruent with the difference in semiotic systems. Although nobility and clergy subjected the serfs to the word of Christianity, the religious inscriptions were never fully assimilated into the culture of the illiterate masses. Besides, historical and economic development did not allow for an intermediate zone of culture to develop as rapidly as it did in the western part of the European continent. Trade and printing technology initiated the consolidation of the middle classes by the sixteenth century in the West, while the Slavic feudal lords actively worked to destroy the bourgeoisie in East-Central Europe.[4] The region remained locked in a binary model of cultural identity, constructing a peculiar model of "for or against" ideology and the already proverbial Slavic extremism both in politics and culture.

dualism and identity

The Old Bulgarian apocryphal legend cited in the epigraph illustrates one of the most important aspects of the pagan culture that has survived within the dominant order of Christianity: both God and devil emerged from the water, the feminine element that preceded the creation of the world. The differentiation of cultural opposites was made possible after the separation from the common mythological source, through the division of the element that is identified with the maternal. The construction of this binary opposition rested on the ability of the new, Christian culture to transform this maternal element (commonly identified with the mythic elements of water and earth) into a dark, threatening force, while positing itself as the representative of light and progress. God was also supported by the institution of writing, while the devil remained tied to illiteracy and the undifferentiated, yet powerful, feminine element. This dark, obverse side of Slavic cultural identity acted as an unconscious structure that is retained and reinscribed within the dual structure found through a wide range of non-Christian practices.

Yuri Lotman, who treats culture as a collective mechanism for the storage and processing of information, has recognized the importance of the dual model in the semiotic organization of early Russian culture.[5] Since the Eastern Slavic and the Orthodox part of the South Slavic culture retained the dark, maternal element in a particularly marked form, Lotman refrains from applying the dual model to the semiotic study of Western Slavic cultures (Czechs, Poles, Slovaks, Croats, Slovenes), which developed under the influence of Catholicism. But, although the Catholic church was politically more successful in its fight against the native mythemes, it did not completely eradicate the opposition, which was preserved in the zone of subculture. The dark side of Slavic mythology erupted in the Bogumil teachings from the Balkan region, which manifested a powerful residual anti-Christian dimension among the illiterate masses.[6]

The apocryphal version of genesis becomes understandable when we turn to its pre-Christian version. According to the oldest Slavic legends, the world was created and ruled by Byelobog, god of light,

day, and life, and by Chernobog, god of darkness, night, and death.[7]
After the establishment of Christianity, this mythic cosmogony was transformed into the apocryphal story about God and devil, who created the world together. This dichotomy underlay the earliest known Slavic mythemes and formed the foundation for all of the subsequent semiotic systems. Another pair of oppositions associated with the dual principle is the high-low distinction: the white god belonged to the divine heights and the sun, while the black god lived in the depths of earth or water. The gender distinctions between the two gods were not manifested in the original cosmogony since they symbolized the concrete, physical elements, abstracted from the observable natural and social phenomena. But the worship of Mati-Syra-Zemlya (Moist Mother Earth) by the peasants until this day points to the association of the feminine element with the dark, diabolical side of the dualistic deity.[8]

The originary binary oppositions were the echoes of the clash between the written word and the dominantly oral discursive practices. The spoken word and the carved image were the primary forms of cultural representation used by the ancient Slavs. Christianity brought a more advanced technological tool: the written word was capable of uniting the orthographic image of the letter and the spoken word of oral culture into a single unit of meaning. Literacy was a more efficient medium of social control than the oral tradition, providing for the legal foundations of the medieval Slavic states. Since Christianity was first accepted by the nobility in order to adapt to Western standards of civilization, writing practices in the Slavic world were engendered in the socially privileged area of "high culture."

The first texts in the Slavic world were translations of Christian literature from Greek and Latin, the written word of foreign origin that came to represent "high" cultural values, functionally replacing the old pagan idols, which derived from the Indo-European worship of the white sun god (Svarog, Pyerun)[9] The idol of the pagan god of the "high region" was replaced by the Holy Sign and by the religious icon; at the same time, the spoken word of pagan origin was relegated to the realm of illiterate culture. During the medieval period, subcultural values continued to survive among the lower, peasant classes, even as these values run parallel to the consecrated texts of the

Church and the nobility, preserving an abundance of unofficial, distorting, and parodic ritual forms. This subterranean reservoir of unofficial culture survived under different cultural guises until the twentieth century, when the so-called "dissidents" came to occupy the "low" position within the dual model.

Literate culture in the medieval period was immediately associated with the word of the Christian God, with the iconic values that presumed to inscribe an absolute spiritual essence and to occupy the space of truth and justice. Because the word of God was imposed from above, from the realm of aristocracy and church fathers, it corresponded to the pagan belief in the white god, who was associated with the light, sun, and the higher social classes. The other realm, associated with the darkness, earth, and water in the popular imagination, was represented within Christianity by the figure of the devil, who belonged to the space of nonculture or subculture and was condemned by the clergy as the world of the pagan past, of the demonic present, or of an apocalyptic future. Those three temporal codings of the "dark realm" were possible only after the introduction of the Judeo-Christian idea of the linear and progressive course of time and history, which was superimposed over the pagan belief in the cyclical recurrence of seasons.

The new, linear conception of history imported with Christianity enabled the Slavs to construct a myth about their detachment from paganism and the transformation of the people into the new (Christian) people, who enter the new (historical) period of development. At the same time, Slavic cultures inscribed their own pagan heritage within the imported system of writing as a negative value that was nevertheless retained inside the system. This negative value erupted in numerous pagan practices that were preserved in Slavic popular culture long after the "break" with the pagan past. Lotman and Uspenski see a manifestation of the "ancient element" in various practices: until the sixteenth century peasants buried their dead in burial mounds rather than in consecrated cemeteries; sexual orgies in honor of the pagan god Kupalo persisted until the eighteenth century; and certain features of the pagan wedding were restored immediately following the October Revolution of 1917. Šermeteva gives an example of a wedding that took place right after the Revolution:

"There were cases when a couple wishing to avoid a church wedding was afraid to tell their parents about this. They would travel a few miles away from the village as if they were going to church in a neighboring village, but before reaching it they would stop in the woods, get off the cart, and go around a fir tree with lighted candles."[10]

The young couple was unconsciously reviving the ancient Slavic wedding ritual by dancing around a fir tree. This shows the further revival of pagan practices after the October Revolution had officially dethroned the Christian Orthodoxy in Russia. Lotman's analysis shows how various conceptions of history, combined with the ideology of progress, led to the return of ancient cultural forms, while the culture consciously experienced the detachment from the old and the assimilation of the new. He explains this by a lack of an intermediary, neutral zone in the Russian medieval conception of afterlife:

> Discussion of a particular case will make clear what we have in view: in the Catholic Christian West, life after death is divided into three zones: paradise, purgatory and hell. Similarly, life on earth is thought of as demonstrating three kinds of behavior: definitely sinful, definitely holy and a neutral kind which permits salvation beyond the grave after an ordeal in purgatory. Again, in the actual life of the medieval West we find a wide brand of neutral behavior and there are neutral social institutions which are neither "holy", nor "sinful", neither "state organized", nor "anti-state", they are neither good nor bad. . . . The Russian medieval system was constructed on a marked dualism. To continue our example, we find that the Russian system divides life after the grave into heaven and hell. There is no provision for an intermediate zone. And correspondingly, behavior in this life is either sinful or holy. This dualism extends also to concepts unconnected with the Church. Secular authorities might be regarded as divine or demonic, but never as neutral in relation to these concepts.[11]

The lack of a neutral, intermediate zone of cultural values makes it impossible for the course of history to perform a complete break with the old and achieve a qualitatively new stage in the future. The category of the new does not emerge from the value-neutral cultural reserve. Although "neutrality" is itself a fairly problematic concept, it shows the extent to which the Slavic world was retarded by its inability to allow for the development of the middle classes which, according to Peter Bürger, are responsible for the development of "autonomous" cultural practices.[12]

The autonomy of the bourgeois work of art has a strong negative connotation in Bürger's *Theory of the Avant-Garde,* demonstrating the differences in the historical and cultural forces that influence the Western half and the Eastern half of Europe. While the West tried to overcome the autonomy of the work of art and make it a part of the mysterious "life process," the East struggled to break the work of art's ties with despotic political power to achieve an "autonomy" and, through a paradoxical validation of the "purely artistic" value of writing practices, to abandon the vicious circle of the dual model. According to Lotman and Uspenski, the new always incorporates the elements of the old, but with a negative sign. "In this way repeated changes could in fact lead to the regeneration of archaic forms."[13] Every time history makes a break with the "old ways" in order to embody a new stage, it is also, in actual fact, returning in the direction of the old pagan origins. Thus, the reforms under Peter the Great—the so-called Europeanization of Russia in the eighteenth century, which propagated the image of the "new Russia" and saw Russians as the "new people" transformed by the ideals of Western enlightenment—were actually a step backwards, toward the realm of "low" culture:

> The energetic struggle which was carried on by the secular state and the system of education against the Church monopoly in the sphere of culture was suddenly reinterpreted in the mass upper class consciousness as the regeneration of paganism. . . . The subjective "Europeanization" of life had nothing in common with any real convergence with Western lifestyle, and at the same time definitely influenced the setting up of anti-Christian forms such as had certainly never been possible in the life of the Christian West.[14]

One of the significant features of the Petrine epoch was the open organization of serf harems, which became a normal feature of the nobleman's life in the eighteenth century. The "assimilation of European culture" was present only on the surface: the girls selected for the harem had to wear European-style clothes and learned how to read and write. The reversion to pagan polygamy had to be accompanied by an external expression of "progress," manifested in

clothing and literacy of the serf girls. Lotman produces a large variety
of examples to demonstrate the basic operation of the dual model of
culture: ideological repression of one of the components in the
dynamic pair of cultural oppositions led to the vigorous revival of the
opposing tendency. Christianity in Russia was almost a secret force
during the Petrine era, an era that regenerated the ancient pagan
practices under the guise of "Europeanization." Furthermore, the
sociocultural division between the nobility and the serfs was not so
strict after Peter's "Westernization": the higher classes were now "contaminated" with pagan practices that were previously reserved only
for the peasant classes in the illiterate zone of subculture. The resulting interest in the study of Slavic folklore is one of the most important side-effects of this cultural "contamination," which extended
well into the next century. The Orthodox Christian element, which
revived the Slavophile movements in Russia in the nineteenth century, passed through a period of withdrawal from the public sphere
just a century earlier. This era was also of great importance for the
introduction of writing into the secular sphere—the creation of the
modern Russian literary language began under the rule of Peter the
Great. But every act of secular writing was still implicitly understood
as a deviation from the norm, a demiurgic attempt to usurp the position of the "higher language" that was first occupied by Old Church
Slavic or Latin and then by other foreign languages.

So far, this discussion of Slavic culture has been limited to the
Russian element, to the language that preserved most of the archaic
cultural paradigms because of a stronger geopolitical isolation, somewhat greater than that of the rest of the Slavic peoples. The Balkan
peninsula, inhabited by both the Orthodox and the Catholic Slavs,
was prone to a much greater level of cultural hybridization as a result
of invasions, and colonizations, by Germanic, Hungarian, Turkish,
Greek, and Italian forces. The Serbo-Croatian language exhibits the
degree of atomization that the lands of the South Slavs underwent
from the inception of their history. The Serbs and the Croats share a
common language, but are the carriers of two different historical and
religious traditions. Although both nations write in the same language, the Serbs and the Croats use different alphabets. Since the
Croats are predominantly Catholic, they use the Latin orthography,

while the Serbs continue to use the Cyrillic, modernized from Church Slavic. The two nations, which share a common Slavic origin, are divided by the political, historical, and cultural influences that, through the invasion of the various foreign elements, starting with the dissolution of the Roman Empire, have colonized and divided these Slavic tribes from the outside. The effect of colonization on the national identity of Serbs and Croats is perhaps best illustrated by the current war raging in Yugoslavia.

The persistence of the initial Christian model under the Ottoman occupation in Serbia and Bulgaria gave the Holy Sign a slightly different historical coding than it had in Russia: the Orthodox church, in conjunction with the public performances of the oral heroic narratives, became the main axis of popular assembly. Therefore, Christianity and paganism were both relegated to the cultural underground due to Islamic domination: literate culture was not associated exclusively with the socially dominant upper class of Slavic origin, but with the Turkish invaders. There was no possibility for an acute high-low distinction within the same language community, and although Church Slavic was the official language of the Serbian and Bulgarian Orthodox Church, it blended freely with the vernacular idiom, which was linguistically quite similar to it. The "low" popular culture was much closer to the holy, iconic element, thus contributing to a more homogeneous blend of high-low cultures than in the case of Imperial Russia.

The Western Slavs produced a ruling class that was able to maintain illusory distance from the pagan element since it had assimilated Latin and Germanic influences earlier than the rest of the Slavic tribes had. Up to the Renaissance, most of Polish literature was written in Latin. But the illiterate peasant culture preserved most of the ancient Slavic practices since Latin was identified with the realm of the high, literate culture. The era of the humanistic rebirth produced the first works in the Polish vernacular tongue. The gap between high and low cultures was almost as drastic as it was in Russia: Poland produced codes of knightly behavior, honor connected with aristocratic signs (name, title, rank), and, most important of all, the rights of the feudal master. All of these practices required the operation of literate functions, which were used to divide and distinguish the nobility from the majority of the population.

The population of all the Slavic territories continued to share a common cultural pattern that was limited to the peasant classes within the cultural underground. Placed in the abject position of serfs, the Slavic peasantry preserved most of the pagan models, which survived side by side with official Christian culture. Whether Orthodox or Catholic, the lower classes, which have not had the access to literacy, could only worship God and his literate world in the position once functionally occupied by Byelobog. That realm was associated with the world of the masters, with the high and mighty, with the sun and God the Father. But there was also the sphere of existence that tied the lower classes to the realm of earth, a concrete material connection with the dark, feminine element. This connection preserved an abundance of magical and sacrificial practices that were often closely connected to the body and its "shameful" functions. From the point of view of high, Christian culture, these practices were demonic and blasphemous.

The dominant ritual practice among Slavic peasantry was the circle dance, exemplified by *kolo* of the Slavic peasantry in the Balkans. *Kolo* not only countered the linear structure of Christian mass and liturgy, but also provided a cultural space for the expression of the other, "unofficial" side of life. Vuk Karadžić writes about an event in nineteenth-century Serbia, which surprised him with its boldness. He describes a scene in which the Turkish lords "sit on the ground, while the Serbs around them dance and declaim." One of the songs was aimed at the masters at the realm of power occupied by Turkish feudal lords:

Hoot, holler, today, tomorrow
Our feet, Turkish soil;
But the Turks don't give a damn;
Mighty lords eat shit,
And their helpers
wipe the master's plates [15]

Everything was allowed during the circle dance: all prohibitions were lifted and the high, serious, despotic values were mocked and cursed. This was the practice that turned against the hegemonic in politics, history, and culture, affirming the truth of the body from the low-culture point of view. This alternative truth distorted the "official" vision of the world and shattered the cultural order derived from the higher world of literacy, seriousness, and power. Mikhail Bakhtin's analysis of the Western Renaissance culture draws on this aspect of Slavic popular cultures, which had been reduced to a low and abject status by the dominant power exactly because they reminded the high and official culture, supported by Tsar, Church, or Party, of its origins in the "low" cultural element.

slavdom and modernity

The sixteenth century marks a turning point in the development of East-Central Europe and Russia. The regions of Europe inhabited by the Slavs became culturally more and more detached from developments in the materially more productive countries of Western Europe. The ancient and medieval models of Slavic culture resisted the "modernization" of European consciousness that emerged with the strengthening of the middle classes and the ideology of liberal humanism. While the binary universe was challenged in the West with the emergence of the bourgeoisie, dualism is actually invigorated in the East, with its rigid cultural coding of high/low, new/old, and good/bad dichotomies. This development was supported by the revival of the feudal system and the institution of "second serfdom." Although wealthy peasant sons attended Polish universities in the sixteenth century and Jan Huss led the Czechs in a first proto-Protestant uprising against the corrupt Catholic leaders in the fifteenth, the feudal order asserted its dominance over all spheres of social and political life by the end of sixteenth century in the region. The only exception to this may have been the rise of secular humanism in Bohemia and Moravia, where the Hussite movement prepared the ground for the later rapid development of middle-class culture in the nineteenth century. Poland was independent, but failed to produce an urban class like the one that was promoting doctrines of social progress in the West. While Russia stood on the heights of Ivan the Terrible's despotism and viewed itself as the "Third Rome," the South Slavs endured the Ottoman domination. This historical decline had a lasting effect on the development of cultural institutions and literature.

The "rift" between the cultures of Western Europe, which managed to develop the concept of "autonomous" culture, and the "other" Europe, which did not manage to do so until the eighteenth and nineteenth centuries, was responsible for the abundance of revolutionary rhetoric that later occupied the best minds of the region. The political situation of the "other" Europe at the dawn of the modern age was characterized by the despotic domestic rulers or by foreign occupation. The culture that developed in the enclaves of the courts usually had decorative or ecclesiastical functions, while the culture of the serf classes retained its oral and ritualistic character. The self-perception of Eastern European intelligentsia was almost without exception infused with the residues of material lack and the fact of technological backwardness. Although these intellectuals were now the carriers of literate culture, their position was already borderline within the dual model of Slavic culture. Their literacy was infused with opposition and negativity, since their education did not permit the acceptance of Christian dogmas at face value. Because the educated classes generally graduated from Western universities, they brought back home a specific inferiority complex, which gradually developed into a messianic political and cultural mission. The only hope was seen in catching up with the more developed West through political change, which was articulated in the rhetoric of "rebirth," "awakening," "resurrection," and finally "revolution."

The historical division of Europe and the emergence of nationalism as an ideology contributed to the further confusion of Slavic cultural identity. Imperial Russia became the major colonial power in the region, while the rest of the Slavic world ended up divided between the Habsburg and Ottoman empires. The pattern of acculturation present in the Middle Ages was repeated: the ideas of Enlightenment were received from a foreign (French, German, or English) culture and were assimilated and hybridized within the particular Slavic context. This was also the period when most of the

Slavic countries developed literary languages in the modern sense of the word, remodeling the Church Slavic and Latin alphabets in order to adapt them to the vernacular speech. This may seem to have been a sign of approximation between the "high" and "low" cultures, but it in fact only indicated the regrouping of hegemonic forces. Peasants were still politically oppressed, in spite of the emerging interest in the folklore they were seen to be producing.

Also, this was the age when Western romantics (Herder, Mérimée, Goethe) began to "discover" and to glorify the folk cultures as an affirming force that had sprung from the reservoir of the oral tradition. As usually happens with "discoveries" of this kind, the "natural Slav" turned out to be a variation on the noble savage myth: the peasants were portrayed as happy folk living in harmony with nature, untouched by the alienating artifice of civilization. As the ideology of aestheticism gradually became the dominant force in modern Western culture, the romantics appropriated the myth of the "natural man" as a tool for opposing the utilitarian perspective of the "official," who supported the enlightened despotism of the state and its institutions.

This descent into the realm of "low culture" gradually engendered the revolutionary ideology of the Slavic intelligentsia during the nineteenth century. The literate minority that was not directly tied to the Church and to the state began to identify with the serfs and their social position, calling for the political and social equality of all human beings. Most of the Slavic romantics advocated the emancipation of the serfs, the national liberation of the conquered Slavic countries, and a pan-Slavic reunion. The literary values of classicism were turned upside down, and the resurgence of the "demonic" cultural elements became more and more prominent. Kajetan Koźmian, one of the Polish writers who strongly rejected the "new" values of the romantics by defending classicism and the world of the masters, expressed his disgust with the poetics that was being contaminated by the "low" cultural element:

> Don't learn, rather write as you desire. . . . Let us rip up the rules of poetics. . . . Let us sit ourselves down, lute in hand, among the village spinners, and, in their folk language, create new standards, let us sing the

praises of witches, horrors, sorcerers, and ghosts. . . . These base themes provide enough rhymes as a foundation. What difference does it make that they stink a bit? After all they're national! The base object is worthy of poet's song. . . . Everything is beautiful in nature and worthy of being seen and heard, the good horse just as beautiful as the swamp toad. . . . Greetings happy age that has grounds for being proud, you will be capable of giving us nature's true picture; hasten upon the stage to present our growing hopes: the magnificent robbers, the noble criminals. . . . Who could not succumb to such wonders? However, not God, but Satan has created such poets! [16]

Kožmian's satirical piece bears witness to the public perception of the romantic writer—he is the creation of Satan because he is associated with the "base object" that belongs to the "stinking" world of peasants. What is striking in this citation is the inability to step outside Christian dualism even when a critical statement about literature is being made: Kožmian characterized the romantic poet as the creation of Satan, not as a political revolutionary nor as an artistic innovator. The "dark" element is coded both in terms of the class position and in terms of the aesthetic experience from Kožmian's point of view—it violates the classical insistence on the beauty and precision of the rational and formal elements of artistic practice, the harmony of a universe created by God and supported by the feudal order.

The romantic period provided a context for the assimilation of the "low" cultural element into the literate universe, gradually transforming it into the artistic practice that later became dominant in modernist literature. Kožmian's perception of Slavic romanticism as a contamination of writing by elements from a nonculture of "village spinners and their folk language" manifests the degree of ongoing separation between the two cultural zones. The uncanny and estranged world of romantic literary notions is spiced with nationalism that searches for its roots among the peasantry whose "base themes stink a bit." The writer's task was no longer restricted to the creation of beautiful worlds for the entertainment of nobility; the Slavic writer of the romantic period was inspired by the messianic spirit of the revolutionary age and saw himself as the carrier of progress and emancipation for the people.

This age eventually culminated in the abolition of serfdom and in the birth of national consciousness. The writing practices gained more autonomy from the Church, while the state devised a system of secular censorship that was supposed to keep the "demonic" element of the new, disruptive poetic practices in check. The nineteenth century prepared a way for the twentieth-century revolutions through a variety of intellectual movements that questioned and attacked the existing political and social order: the traditionally sanctified values of autocracy and religion gave way to the ideology of nationalism and liberalism. Russian populists and nihilists were probably the best examples of the messianic tendency inherent in this transformation: all of their efforts were directed against the "higher realm" of monarchy and were carried out in the name of the people. The revolutionary idealism of the age and the uncritical faith in the ability of the intellectuals to initiate a positive social change eventuated in the October Revolution. The Russian religious philosopher Nikolai Berdyaev analyzed the messianic dimension of Slavic ideology:

> The Russian people, in full accordance with their particular mentality, offered themselves as a burnt-offering on the altar of an experiment unknown to previous history: they have demonstrated the most extreme consequences of certain ideas. They are an apocalyptic people and they could not stop short at a compromise, some "humanitarian state:" they had to make real either brotherhood in Christ or comradeship in Antichrist. If the one does not reign, then the other will. The people of Russia have put this choice before the whole world with awe-inspiring force.[17]

The extreme projection of "German ideology" imported through the writings of Hegel, Schelling, and ultimately Marx resulted in an extreme version of "Slavic ideology." Berdyaev's perception of the choice between the "brotherhood in Christ" and the "comradeship in Antichrist" demonstrated the marked dualism present in the way every change and revolutionary transformation in the Slavic world was perceived and interpreted. Dualism does not permit for an intermediary, "humanitarian" solution, but always executes an idea with extremism, which often turns the idea into its opposite.

The Russian Revolution of 1917 unleashed the cultural forces that were repressed but dormant among the uneducated and illiterate masses. The awakening of those forces during the October Revolution, the rebellion against the Tsar and the Church who were brought down from the "high" position of power and divine authority is a metaphor for a cultural regression to the pre-Christian Slavic world. The official atheism reinforced and legitimated this tendency by removing the regulative mechanism that the clerical institutions enforced through the Christian religion. The new totalitarian society emerged as a return to the world of paganism, a fact manifested in the substitution of the Christian cross with a symbol of the red star, which was associated with occult, non-Christian practices.

Immediately after the October Revolution, the new poetics engendered by the Russian artistic avant-garde expressed this insurrection against the pre-revolutionary world of "high" cultural norms. The desire to return to a "natural state of language" after the revolution by abolishing the arbitrariness of the sign and restoring it to a relationship of full identification with the revolutionary process was a sign of rebellion against writing as an institution of high culture. Futurist verse demonstrated the tendency of return to more archaic layers of culture and consciousness that, it was hoped, would transcend the original imposition of Christian rationality on artistic practice through *zaum,* a so-called trans-sense language. According to Yuri Tinyanov, Khlebnikov's "pagan attitude regarding words" manifested itself in onomatopoeias and glossolalias, which were an attempt to re-oralize the written language.[18] In the case of Mayakovsky there was a direct rebellion of the poet against the sun, against the realm of light, against the high cultural values:

one more minute
and you will meet
the monarch of the skies
if I want, I'll kill him for you, the sun![19]

Mayakovsky voiced the imaginary power of the "new man," a poet who has created himself through the revolutionary process and who aspires to kill the sun, a symbol of the hegemony of light over the regions of darkness populated by the people. The sun was equated with the monarch, with the "old world" of Tsarism, which was sacrificed for the sake of the revolution. The return to pre-Christian imagery and the insistence on rhythm and the dynamics of verse reinforced cultural dualism: the leap into the "new" society was actually a regeneration of more archaic forms of signification. The dark element was liberated from the unconscious, and the unleashed semiotic forces were believed to "tear the word" and detach it from its "old" meanings. Throughout the 1920s, the Russian literary scene was dominated by the avant-gardist search for a new, revolutionary art. The dream of breaking away from the world of the old and corrupt culture, the invention of the new man and the new language, led to a revival of more primitive forms of expression. The invention of *zaum,* a poetic language that transcended the common-sense boundaries of everyday speech, led literary practice into the realm of pure subjectivity. Russian Formalists saw old literary language as something petrified by tradition and convention that should be refreshed by leaping into the new, revolutionary reality. This attitude was articulated in the domain of poetics as the futurist new primitivism.

Contrary to their intention, the work of avant-garde artists became less and less understandable to members of the social strata beyond the circles of the intelligentsia. For that reason, the work of the avant-garde became suspect within the the new society whose program was based on egalitarian ideology and collectivist communality. The consolidation of "realist" forces triumphed only a decade later, with the enforcement of the socialist realist doctrine. The official suppression of the avant-garde marked a drastic reversal inside the dual model, with Party taking the place that the Church had occupied during the Middle Ages. This is how Ždanov defined the doctrine of socialist realism in 1934: "Socialist Realism, the basic method employed by the Soviet artistic literature and literary criticism, demands from the writer an authentic, historically specific depiction of reality in its revolutionary development. This authenticity and historical specificity in the depiction of reality should be combined with the task of ideologically reshaping and educating the toilers in the spirit of socialism."[20]

The avant-gardist experiments were abandoned and once more repressed into the zone of nonculture. Ždanov's decree of socialist realism demanded that the writer conform to the Party platform in the same way the Christian monk had had to respect the theological canon. In addition to following the absolute mimetic projection of reality designed by the Party ideologists, the writer is obliged to embody the attitude of "revolutionary romanticism," always plotting a positive outcome that will be conveyed to his "readers-toilers" and thus will motivate them to ever greater efforts in the building of the new socialist order. The socialist realist method established three fundamental rules, whose function was reminiscent of the Holy Trinity for the medieval man: *narodnost*—a sense of belonging to the people and of being their spokesman, which will protect the writer against any tendency to stray into subjective and individualistic perceptions of "socialist reality"; *ideynost*—literature should espouse a definite set of ideas that reflect the mature ideological setup of the socialist realist writer, who is himself a toiler within the socialist community; and *partiynost*—the writer should reflect the current Party policy through his own artistically elaborated vision of reality.

The rules that the politician devised for the writer were a manifestation of a compulsive desire of the Party leadership to maintain control over every aspect of social life. It is not necessary to prove how counterrevolutionary this practice turned out to be. The revolution of literary forms initiated by the avant-garde was suppressed by the demand from the political office: the word had to be defended against its politically incorrect, dangerous, or ambiguous usages.

The first result of the socialist realist campaign was a restoration of the literary methods of realism and the narrative structures of the Slavic heroic epic. The new hero of socialist labor possessed all the qualities of the folk hero of the Slavic oral epic, resituated in a new, revolutionary context of class struggle and material renovation. The political demand produced a novel that was highly formulaic and lacked the dialogic dimension that, according to the Bakhtin school, distinguishes the novel from the epic.[21] The socialist realist novel actually turned into a socialist realist epic, foregrounding a hero who inhabits the realm of absolute epic distance—he is bound to always emerge as the victor in the face of all social, historical, and political odds. The action of the novel usually developed within the single, one-dimensional foreground that insured the repetition of all the stages in the hero's progress—emergence from the people to defend their interest, confrontation with the reactionary forces, and the final conquest of corruption, which leads to the hero's insight into the nature of revolutionary life and reality.

Thus, in the thirties, socialist realist novels portrayed the struggle of the working class hero who overcomes selfishness and corruption and finds truth by serving the people. But, by the forties, the socialist realist novel was transformed into a thoroughly neoclassical ode to the working class. These were the tales of working-class dynasties, existing in a world of perfect harmony between the natural and the social. The elements of heroism and class struggle were slowly toned down, since the new Stalinist order did not need any more revolutionary rhetoric to embed itself in the position of power.[22] The whole project of socialist realist literature became a part of the process of social engineering, which was supposed to inject certain ideals into the toiler's mind and to inspire him on the way to the glorious society of the future. The medieval origin of such a practice is obvious: the "high" Party ideals were glorified by the writer and the artist for the ideological education of the masses. The main revolutionary ideal, the creation of a classless society, gradually vanished from literature, as the Party and its officials assumed the dominant role, which was functionally similar to that of the feudal lords. During the Great Purges, Stalin showed how this "higher" realm of political power could turn into its opposite, with demonic consequences. Apart from the genocide of millions, the Stalinist era had a lasting crippling effect on the development of Russian literature and culture. The insistence on representing "socialist reality in its revolutionary development" eliminated from the literature the uncanny, the inner exploration, which was labeled as reactionary, bourgeois, and degenerate. Therefore, the nineteenth-century tradition, which culminated in the novels of Dostoyevski, the Symbolists, and the works of the twentieth-century avant-garde—and their imaginative exploration of inner landscapes—was gradually eradicated during this period.

The ideology of socialist realism, which saw itself as an ideology of revolution, achieved its theoretical apotheosis in the critical work of Georg Lukács, who vigorously attacked "the ideology of modernism"

because it destroyed the "unity of the world," which was always perceived by the realist writer as "a living whole inseparable from man
himself." He accused the modernist writers of morbid concern with
psychopathology, which according to Lukács, originated in the basic
experience of alienation and in the extreme individualism of the
bourgeois writer. The demand for health was always dominant in
revolutionary ideology, and Lukács espoused that demand in the field
of literary criticism. "Socialist realism is able to portray from inside
the human beings whose energies are devoted to the building of a
different future, and whose psychological and moral make-up is
determined by this."[23] Lukács revealed the Hegelian-Marxist subtext
of this illusory realism that tacitly assumed the absolute and objective
existence of disembodied revolutionary ideals. But in material reality,
Ždanov's demand for *ideynost* turned socialist realism into the opposite of the accurate representation of reality and its contradictions,
since it actually only restated the basic assumptions of Platonic idealism. "The building of a different future" was determined by the program of the Communist Party, which was established as the ideal
value (of the same axiological status as Plato's ideas) toward which the
new revolutionary reality was to be constructed. *Partiynost, Ideynost,*
and *Narodnost* replaced the classical Platonic ideas of the True, the
Good, and the Beautiful in the cultural space that was previously
inhabited by the Christian Trinity (Father, Son, and the Holy Spirit)
since the Middle Ages.

The eruption of the pagan element in the works of the avant-garde
was suppressed by the despotic hierarchy of the Stalinist era. Once
more, the ideals of the "bright" future were re-established in the
sphere of the high, now, socialist culture. The dark, demonic determinant of Russian culture was officially repudiated and exiled into
the cultural underground. After the enforcement of socialist realism,
the dissident artist started bearing the label that functionally originated in the realm of pre-Christian culture. Dualism was now
reflected (in the sphere of cultural politics) in the opposition between
the institutional writers and intellectual dissidents. But, apart from
dissidents who embraced the ideology of realism and wished to
oppose the Party by desiring power and historical truth by employing

introduction

modes of representation similar to those of socialist realism (e.g., Solzhenitsyn, Ćosić), there is a specific type of fiction that continued the literary revolution initiated by the avant-garde, only by different means.

What I propose to call borderline poetics originated in the desire of the writer to reclaim the sphere of language for his own, often narcissistic, purposes in order to articulate his vision on the margins between the artifices of identity and the malignancies of ideology, while giving expression to the dissolution of "reality" constructed by socialist realism and other realisms. The recent events that shook the Communist world under the slogans of *glasnost* and *perestroika* will pose a significant challenge to the dual model. The quick arrival and even quicker departure of Mikhail Gorbachev functionally represents a fusion of the liberal reforms of Peter the Great and Lenin's Communist revolution. Gorbachev's role of the "Good Tsar" who fights bureaucratic corruption, champions freedom of artistic expression, and allows the countries of the Soviet bloc to decide the course of their own destinies has provoked a response from the other side of the cultural continuum. Various nationalist awakenings throughout the Slavic world are an ominous reminder that the dualism is alive and well at the end of the twentieth century.

The rejection of the Stalinist past uncannily resembles the negation of the pagan heritage after the introduction of Christianity or the negation of Christianity after the October Revolution. It is not then unusual that Christianity is now again officially recognized as the legitimate way of expressing one's religious feelings. The radical denial of the past as "negative" and the glorification of the future as "positive" seems to be obligatory in order to create an impression of "progress." This political change has permitted the development of the long-awaited "autonomy" of culture from ideology. However, this autonomy need not be equated with alienation, since culture and politics will probably remain in close proximity to each other. The role of the intellectuals in the overthrow of repressive governments throughout Eastern Europe and the election of the playwright Václav Havel as president of Czechoslovakia are just further evidence of how vital the influence of culture on politics can be in the "lands-in-between." But a real danger is posed by the resurgence of nationalist

borderline poetics

The authors who embrace the borderline poetics are concerned with
ways in which ideology and identity relate to each other after the rise
of totalitarianism in twentieth-century Europe and the Soviet Union.
Their extreme individualistic orientation originates in the rejection
of the ideologies (Nazism and communism) that have attempted to
change the course of European history and fashion the "new man."
These historical forces use ideology to construct an image of human
identity that is based entirely on the ability of the subjects of these
historical forces to conform and serve the political power. The realistic novel is the best formal mode for the enforcement of such ideological visions, since it treats literary language as a transparent
medium for the transmission of desired meanings. On the other
hand, experimental prose questions the limits of realism and examines the effects ideology has on the formation of identity. It is bound
to be seen as something demonic, sick, or subversive by those who
control the discourse of ideology, since it portrays the marginal
nature of the human condition and rejects both the average citizen
and the idealized leader. In the thirties, the Nazis, as well as the
Stalinists, lead a relentless campaign against what they called "degenerate" art. Adolf Hitler himself voiced this demand for the
purification of the German *Volk* body from "that flood of slime and
ordure" that was engendered during the Weimar republic:

> I have observed among the pictures submitted here, quite a few paintings
> which make one actually come to the conclusion that the eye shows
> things differently to certain human beings than the way they really are,
> that is, that there really are men who see the present population of our
> nation only as rotten cretins . . . Either these so-called "artists" really see
> things this way and therefore believe in what they depict; then we would
> have to examine their eye-sight deformation to see if it is the product of a
> mechanical failure or of inheritance. In the first case, these unfortunates
> can only be pitied . . . If, on the other hand, they themselves do not

believe in the reality of such impressions but try to harass the nation with this humbug for other reasons, then such an attempt falls within the jurisdiction of the penal law.[24]

Hitler was probably the most extreme example of an ideologist who wanted to appropriate art for his own political purposes. Every artefact that calls into question the established laws of perception and unsettles the viewer's conception of a stable and dependable reality is seen as a threat to the dominant political order and is portrayed as pathology—to be cured by the doctor or to be imprisoned by the policeman. It is not accidental that the ideology of Lukács and the ideology of Hitler, apparently on two ends of the political spectrum, converge when it comes to the question of literature's social role. The literary artist is supposed to project healthy national ideals that serve as the models for the identification of the masses. Any distortion of the politically constructed "reality" is seen as a usurpation of power, as a move to corrupt and distort the ideological vision that the official art is supposed to project.

Borderline poetics does not experiment with writing, as Khlebnikov, Joyce, or Artaud did, by dismembering logical and narrative structures in order to produce a "new language" that stylistically transcends the boundaries of realistic literary genres. The style of these writers seems "normal" on the surface, while it disturbs the reader on other, less conscious, levels. This apparent "normality" is one of the reasons I have chosen to call their style borderline, since like a borderline personality, it hides a deep existential anxiety under a surface of an ostensibly inconspicuous facade. Borderline poetics uses a range of available narrative discourses (fictional, philosophic, critical) as a *mis en scène* for the articulation of the novelistic vision, which is rooted in an "inner" landscape of contradiction, conflict, and general nonagreement with the ideologically engineered "reality." The literary character is hollowed out and drained of any of the "psychological" content that characterizes the protagonists of realistic novels. In other words, the literary character is a representation of a being unable to construct its own thoughts, feelings, and instincts. Human beings are the products of an ideology that is not consciously embraced, yet that continues to direct and control their destiny. They are one-dimensional representations of undigested ideology that signal the end of humanism. Protagonists are transformed into vehicles for the elaboration of certain existential postures of an (usually negative) ideal. The character is a theatrical mask, a cipher, and a mark constructed by the author in order to illustrate the universe, which is actually a projection of his own pseudo-ontological vision of the human condition. The novel is transformed into a deliberate artifice that simulates the creation of human destiny by the dominant ideologies of the time, a fact that enables borderline fiction to be closer to the Real than the various forms of realism.[25]

Writers of this orientation oppose the absolutist character of the ideals proclaimed by the literary programs of the socialist realist type by parodying those ideals and showing their effects on the prosaic level of actuality. The writer reflects the results of ideological devastation without direct critical engagement, which he views as heavy-handed and vulgar. There is often a lack of critical distance from that which is criticized in borderline fiction, a fact that can often confuse the reader who is not familiar with the political and historical situation of the writer and his work. The writer manifests the contradictory, irrational side of human existence, producing a poetics of the novel based on fractures. Borderline fiction sets itself against the simplified truths proposed by the political party in order to counter and demystify the "high" revolutionary ideals. This literature is extremely anti-revolutionary, guided by the desire of its creators for personal authenticity and therefore inherently doomed to fall into the early existentialist illusion of non-commitment. Since the escape from one ideology can only become another form of ideology, the writer often creates a literary universe where ideological postures are exposed and left suspended, without a sense of closure that will allow for an easy identification and choice between the opposing sides. This device is a desperate attempt to break away from the constraints of the culturally dominant dualism through a parodic transcendence of totalitarianism and a foregrounding of the writer's own individuality. There is often a longing for the older, romantic concept of the autonomous individual resisting the totalitarian "reality" that threatens to devour him, like an internalized maternal element that dominates the fragile setup of the borderline personality. Although "autonomy of the individual" is a fiction produced by bourgeois culture, borderline poetics attempts to redefine it as a de-massified version of identity in order to elude the totalitarian demand for uniformity and obedience.

The individualistic posturing creates a specific poetics of prose that is borderline in at least three respects. In the first respect, this poetics geo-graphically reflects a collective identity of Slavic peoples who inhabit the borderlands between the Asian cultures in the East and the European culture proper in the West. It is symptomatic of West European ethnocentrism to conceive of the entire Euro-Asian land mass as four Easts (Near, Middle, Far, and Eastern Europe) and only one West, itself. The cultural identity of non-Western Europeans, among whom the Slavs are the largest group, is therefore defined as a lack or negativity that transforms them into secondary Europeans. This attitude of the West often results in national frustrations and cultural inferiority complexes among the secondary Europeans, who attempt to compensate for the lack of proper (Western) culture by trying to be more Western than the West Europeans (e.g., various Anglophiles, Francophiles, etc.) or by being culturally isolated to the point of chauvinism and xenophobia (e.g., Slavophiles). This denial of one's own "easternness" is necessary if the writer is obsessed with getting closer to the West or at least closer to the Center. The concept of Central Europe is a product of this denial, never equal to itself, never able to stabilize culturally, since it perceives itself as a lack. This instability of the political and historical destiny of the region is reflected in the sphere of the personal identity of the writer and his characters. The reader experiences a strong sense of unreality when confronted with these works, since they often invoke the experiences of madness and demonic possession (Bulgakov), psychopathic brutality in the service of politics (Kiš), the abjection of maternal manipulation (Kundera), or the infantile rebellion against all identity (Gombrowicz). None of the writers in this group is interested in "normal" characters, since "normality" constitutes a deviation in the borderline universe.

A second way in which these authors represent a borderline poetics is with regard to the specific identity problem of "other Europeans," caused by historical and political traumas. This identity problem resembles in more than one respect the borderline and narcissistic

personality disorders described in psychopathology.[26] First of all,
there is the metaphoric presence of the controlling mother figure, a
place occupied by the Soviet Empire. This bureaucratic-military
entity is culturally coded as an overprotective feminine presence that
cannot let go of its children both inside and outside the Soviet
Union, rationalizing its domination as love. The effect of this domination is the destruction of all who refused to be loved.[27] The fear of
engulfment by an unknown, terrifying force is a vivid metaphor in the
mind of all the non-Russians, especially Western Slavs. "It is a world
that—provided we are removed from it—intrigues and attracts us;
the moment it closes around us, though, it reveals its terrifying for-
eignness," writes Milan Kundera.[28] The return of pseudo-matriarchy
after the October Revolution is just another cultural coding of Damp
Mother Earth, the mythic feminine presence that is transformed into
the abject power of the Soviet state.

The symbiotic merger with the maternal causes either a narcissistic
rebellion or an ambivalent relationship to femininity (as is the case
with Kundera, Gombrowicz, and Kiš). The case of Bulgakov is
different, since he is directly projecting the maternal domination of
Russian culture through the character of Margarita in *The Master
and Margarita*. However, the borderline cultural identity is in constant danger of being engulfed by the maternal, which threatens the
development of autonomous psychic space. That is one reason why
the characters in borderline fiction resemble puppets, phantoms, and
shadows more than fully developed human beings. They are simula-
tions of identity, "as if" personalities who perform their roles according to the script that has been written for them by an invisible
controlling force. Borderline poetics often reflect this familial
metaphor of the omnipotent mother (of Soviet ideology) and the
absent father (of Christian religion) on the literary level.

The third aspect of borderline poetics is specifically literary and
reflects the tendency of the writer to transcend the boundaries of literary genres and employ philosophical reflections (Kundera), historiographic material (Kiš), theatrical models (Bulgakov), and even
literary criticism (Gombrowicz). Literary genres undergo enjamb-
ment, through the juxtaposition of two or more narrative sequences
without an apparent connection (e.g., the juxtaposition of the

Jerusalem and Moscow narratives in Bulgakov's *The Master and Margarita*.) The novelistic genre is stretched to its limit in order to reflect the changes that have transpired in the realm of history and politics on the formal level. But, far from being serious and moralistic, borderline fiction uses irony, parody, and black humor to exorcise the horrors of political power. This results in a horrible, insane laughter that is a reflection of the madness that has been imposed on the writer by the institutional order. This blending of the horrible and the laughable is a characteristic modernist posture, resulting in the escape from the political sphere, with writing serving as a way of articulating subjectivity and of opposing every ideology.

The parodic positioning and eccentric individuality of the borderline writer could have its origins in the Slavic popular tradition of the holy fool (*urodivoy*).[29] This cultural heritage is an ancient model for the borderline poetics practiced by the intellectual dissident, taking the side of the uncanny, distorted, and abject part of "reality" in order to demonstrate "the unreal, deceptive nature of the external environment." The writer himself feels protected, "encapsulated in a sacred micro-space," because his mission is protected by an order regarded by him as above the laws of the immediate material world ruled by the monolithic ideology. This higher order is constituted by the signifying practice itself, by the freedom that the "play" of language gives him as it converts itself into "reality." The shift of the performative focus (from the performer to the audience) is what causes the problem when the literary performance of the holy fool is transposed into the twentieth century. The one who applies the laws of play in the realm of "socialist reality" is bound to encounter the hard-line border imposed from the outside by the ideologist, who has the power to annihilate every meaning deemed inadmissible from the standpoint of official culture. The dominant cultural practice in socialism insists on an imagination that serves the prescribed social platform of the age, without deviations from the doctrines of verisimilitude and referentiality.

The precursors of borderline fiction are many, with Dostoyevski and Kafka probably the most significant, the former on the eastern border of the region and the latter on the western. They have exerted possibly the greatest influence on twentieth-century artistic writing in general, a period of great internalization, when writing practice starts dissecting the universe within. This tradition, beginning with Dostoyevski, Kafka, and others, is opposed to the dictums of realism, with its glorification of verisimilitude, referentiality, and identification. The practitioners of borderline fiction recast the spirit of the romantic rebellion of the imagination: the writer approaches the Real by distorting reality based on mutual agreement and literary convention. Usually identified as avant-garde or modernist, this literature is driven by the exploration of the other, darker, and lesser-known side of human experience. In order for that de-formed version of reality to emerge, the writer assumes a posture that is marginal and borderline in relation to the univocal version of reality professed by the dominant ideology.

The "reality" Dostoyevski creates through writing is born from the ambivalence in regard to the limits imposed by God's law. The Grand Inquisitor, a literary product of a literary character (Ivan Karamazov), is the incarnation of the ideological apparatus that appropriates and reconstructs the myth of Christ in order to establish totalitarian control over humanity. The institution denies Christ's deeds in order to maintain the domination over the worldly realm. The Grand Inquisitor cynically exploits the faith of his subjects to exercise power and to posit the absolute limit of authority, using Christ as a model for identification that restricts individual freedom. The border between faith and doubt, between Alyosha's and Ivan's versions of reality, manifests the emerging contradictions between the old world of spirituality and the new world of rationality. The latter is seen as a world that denies Christ's love of man as fiction invented by the technologists of human soul like the Grand Inquisitor.

Dostoyevski believes that salvation through loving Christ is a way the world can be saved from the corruption and decay inherent in the doubt that torments Ivan Karamazov. But, for the contemporary writer, who has witnessed the triumph of Grand Inquisitors in the October Revolution and subsequent revolutions, the possibility of religious sublimation is laughable and naive. Christianity is as transparent as any other ideology, its symbols only good as literary material. Bulgakov's Ieshua is already nothing more than a parodic version of Christ, not an absolute model for identification.

Kafka is the other, Western, prophet of the institution, whose labyrinths are as mysterious as God himself. According to Milan Kundera, the world of Kafka's novels reveals the pseudotheological nature of the large bureaucratic machineries that have occupied and ravaged the human soul in the twentieth century. But, unlike Dostoyevski's protagonists, who are torn between the world of God and the world of institution, Kafka's characters are entirely produced by the logic that replaces and assimilates the power of religion. Power is given to history and its forces, which erase the psychic space of the individual and transform it into an absurd search for identity that is irretrievably lost in the labyrinths of the institution. "The hypnotic eye of power, the desperate search for one's own offence, exclusion and the anguish of being excluded, the condemnation to conformism, the phantasmic nature of reality and the magical reality of the file, the perpetual rape of the private life, etc.—all these experiments that History has performed on man in its immense test tubes, Kafka performed (some years earlier) in his novels."[30]

The transpersonal power of history and its institutions is the motivating force of Kafka's writing and one of the main themes of borderline poetics. The genocide of millions who are labeled as racially, socially, and politically different and abject and the advent of two World Wars and the massive technologization of the human mind are a historical backdrop to this poetic approach.

While discussing Kafka, Deleuze and Guattari posit the concept of a minor literature. "Minor literature is completely different; its cramped space forces each individual intrigue to connect immediately to politics."[31] Wherever minor literature turns, it is cornered by politics that reminds it who is actually in charge of reality production. In the process, the subject is subsumed by a bureaucratic superstructure, which forces him to search for his identity. "There isn't a subject; there are only collective assemblages of enunciation, and literature expresses these acts insofar as they're not imposed from without and insofar as they exist only as diabolical powers to come or revolutionary forces to be constructed."[32]

These "collective assemblages" enable Kafka to exteriorate his allegories of human destiny without disintegrating into aestheticism, as

has often happened with other forms of Western avant-gardism.
Since the hegemonic discourse is more conspicuous as the force that
upholds the realm of the high, serious, and official, the prosaists from
this part of the world are able to articulate the negativity that is
brought about by the historical catastrophes of the region in the
twentieth century.

Borderline poetics perpetually questions the limits of identity and
ideology, producing prose that explores the dark, abject side of history, activated by the confrontation of the individual with the institutionalized powers. The border between individuality and bureaucracy,
analyzed already in Balzac, is now dissolved and rendered invisible.
The distance between the individual and the political is rapidly
diminishing, until the subject becomes completely invaded by the
"diabolical powers" or "revolutionary forces." The borderline quality
of this rebellion is determined by the marginal, subversive position
that these authors come to occupy. Milan Kundera, who identifies
himself with the fallen angel in the *Book of Laughter and Forgetting*,
exemplifies the position of the subject unable to stabilize his ideological position and consequently attempting to embody contradictions
in his writing by constantly defamiliarizing and subverting the "reality" consisting of officially approved myths and values. The destruction of humanist ethics, as an autonomous and imperative moral
instance, by the highly programmatic ideologies of Stalinism and
Nazism causes a drastic change in the writing practice of those who
can account for that change on the imaginary level.

bulgakov, gombrowicz, kiš, kundera

Borderline poetics produces an image of reality that is distorted by
the banality of materialism (Bulgakov), by the infantilism of various
ideological masks (Gombrowicz), by the malignancy of politics (Kiš),
or by the abjection of lyricism (Kundera). These literary figures have
all been marginalized by dominant political systems through exile,
censorship, and other subtler forms of oppression. In spite of that
marginalization, they have constructed a poetics of resistance that

employs imaginary means to reflect the uncanny universe of totalitarian control.

Mikhail Bulgakov, in his most famous and controversial novel *The Master and Margarita,* juxtaposes two main storylines: one narrative places the reader in the Moscow artistic circles of the 1930s, which is haunted by Woland, a character of diabolical origin; the other narrative is a fictionalized account of Christ's Passion, written by the Master, who is Bulgakov's alter ego. The Russian Revolution (represented by the Moscow narrative) and the Apocalypse (represented by the Jerusalem narrative) are thus set side by side, as the two moments that mark the end and the beginning of Christianity. The appearance of the demonic gang in Moscow is a sign of the return of a religious universe under a different, negative sign. Bulgakov attempts to reconcile the transcendental reality inherent in Master's madness and Christianity with a demonic parody of Stalinist reality. The vulgar materialism of the socialist world is juxtaposed with the (post)romantic love and faith in the power of literature, which enables the Master to live beyond his physical death. Although highly utopian, Bulgakov's novel manifests the political subtext that is the foundation of his artistic and religious allegories, emerging on the border between the material and spiritual realms of human experience.

The search of *Ferdydurke's* protagonist for a face without a mask demonstrates Witold Gombrowicz's desire to distance himself from the "new faiths" of Nazism and Stalinism, which spread among the Polish youth in the mid 1930s. Johnny Kowalsky is the representative of the generation of "free spirits," caught up in the ideological turmoil that calls for the taking of sides and political differentiation. *Ferdydurke* reflects the extremely politicized "reality" of prewar Poland, which is a source of torment for the protagonist in search of authentic existence. The main character's search for identity turns into a grotesque nightmare. Gombrowicz's character is looking for the pure and sincere essence of his life, only to realize that he is "not expressing himself in harmony with his true nature."[33] Everything that he sees in society is "painfully inflicted on him from outside, either by other men or by circumstances."[34] This novel is prophetic of a stage that Central and Eastern Europe enter in 1937, when the

novel is published. The ideals are being fabricated in the same manner as the cannons and bombs to be used in the pending World War.
Gombrowicz feels that he is living in "the darkest of nights, together
with the whole humanity," which is suffering from a loss of identity
and can see itself only through the mask.[35] This theatricalization of
history and ideology is the motivating force that leads the protagonist
of *Ferdydurke* from the city to the country manor, until he finds some
comfort in the adoration of the "stable lad" and the abduction of his
pale and flaccid cousin.

"The old God was dying," says Gombrowicz in his memoir.[36] His
parody is born as a reaction to the conditions caused by the lifting of
all the sublimatory mechanisms provided by religion. The new political interests produce ideologies that abolish the concept of transcendental truth and embrace the scientific doctrines of progress, paired
with the belief either in the superiority of a race or a collective. The
only position Gombrowicz finds for himself is as the embodiment of
nothingness, the laughable negativity that ridicules the world of ideological values. A desire to escape, to run away from it all and construct a fictional universe that will not support any massive project of
social engineering, to be a person apart from the infantile and highly
ritualized forms of mass behavior (youth marches and parades, uni-
forms, lifestyles) and to affirm an authentic individual position leads
Gombrowicz into dissidence and exile.

Danilo Kiš, in his work *A Tomb for Boris Davidovich*, confronts the
history of the Comintern and the Stalinist period of Russian and East
European history. In the part entitled "The Magic Card Dealing,"
the reader learns about the card game that is called "The Devil or
The Mother." This game determines the destiny and death of innocent Dr. Taube according to the cruel laws of chance in the highly
improbable universe of the Gulag. Kiš's demons are of the most terrifying kind, since they do not find an outlet in the parodic and imaginative distortions of reality, but perform in their own version of
Artaud's theater of cruelty. Kiš appropriates the Borgesian pseudo-
historical poetics in order to expose the powers of horror that inscribe
the official history in the Communist world. The treatment of the
destinies of characters in *A Tomb for Boris Davidovich* shows how

bureaucracy deprives human beings of their dignity, freedom, and ultimately their lives. Kiš employs a quasi-documentary style to provide an alternative to official history, treading a fine line between reality and fiction in order to demonstrate the arbitrariness with which the official historians transform random events of the past into a homogeneous narrative and present it as historical truth. The entire novel reads like a secret, cabalistic archive revealing the tragic destiny of sincere leftist intellectuals and revolutionaries during the Stalinist period.

Milan Kundera's novel *Life Is Elsewhere* takes as its subject the life of a poet in socialist Czechoslovakia in order to criticize and expose what the author calls the lyrical attitude. Lyricism, not only as a literary practice, but also as an existential posture, is a foundation for the development of revolutionary ideology. "Revolution has no need to be examined or analyzed; it only desires that the people merge with it. For that reason, revolutions are lyrical and in need of lyricism."[37] Kundera compares this merger of the people with the revolution to the merger of the poet with his mother, confirming the strong negative coding of the feminine element within the Slavic culture. The mother does not allow the separation and the autonomy of the lyricist; in the same way, the revolution devours the entire person of the revolutionary. Therefore, the lyric poet is seen as the collaborator of totalitarianism, the one who writes odes to the absolute modernity of every revolution. Kundera opposes the values of the lyricist to the values of "the middle-aged man," a bachelor who endures his alienation from the ideologically constructed universe through solitude, meditation, and fornication. On the other hand, the lyricist remains merged with the mother's authority, which makes it easy for him to let go and be embraced by the authority of the state. Again, this negative coding of the feminine unveils the underlying political subtext of Russia as the devouring eastern mother who does not allow her Czech offspring to emerge as independent and autonomous subjects. The mythic underpinnings of totalitarianism with a mother's face are exposed and criticized in a novelistic form, with frequent use of pseudophilosophical discourse that has since become one of the trademarks of Kundera's prose.

The question of the periodization and the sensibility of these works arises almost instantaneously in the mind of the theorist brought up in the recent tradition of Western literary criticism: are they modernist or postmodernist? But a closer look at the political position of Slavic culture makes an easy classification of these authors and novels superfluous. It could be argued that this prose is anti-modernist in its intellectual orientation. Milan Kundera criticizes the "modern art that, in lyrical ecstasy, identifies with the modern world."[38] The relativism of borderline poetics cannot uncritically identify with Rimbaud's poetic imperative to be absolutely modern. "Glorification of the technical, fascination with the future" are the premises of modern sensibility.[39] On the other hand, these writers oppose every absolutist, programmatic and exalted vision of the future in order to place their works on the border between ideology and silence, calling into question almost every horizon of human destiny in the twentieth century.

The writer of this orientation positions himself within the dark, repressed side of the ancient Slavic cultural heritage in order to restore the balance disturbed by the ideologist of the "high and bright" faith in the future. However, this apocalyptic dimension is not somber but comical, recalling Ionesco's words about "a thin line between the horrible and the comic."[40] In attempting to provide a psychopolitical context for these authors and their works, my reading winds along that invisible borderline of poetic difference and traces the articulations of thought and subjectivity that record the alienation, dehumanization, and the forgetfulness of being in twentieth-century Slavic culture.

Mikhail Bulgakov:

Gnosis, Power, and Writing

in *The Master and Margarita*

The Master and Margarita is a novel about the tragic destiny of writers within the context of the new Soviet society. It is not accidental that Mikhail Bulgakov wrote it between 1924 and 1940, during the first sixteen years of Stalin's rule. The novel's poetic credo is engendered by Bulgakov's imaginary rebellion against the official establishment, which enforced a rigid, vulgar materialist version of Marxism during this period of Soviet history. The novel could not be published after the triumph of socialist realism, a literary doctrine that reflected the general trend in Soviet society in the 1930s. The arts were forced to completely identify themselves with the ruling ideology and give up their aesthetic autonomy and status of a powerful social force that the literary avant-garde had achieved by the 1920s.

It was not until November of 1966 that the first part of the novel appeared in the the literary periodical *Moskva*. The entire edition of 150,000 copies, together with the 1967 printing of the second part, was sold out within hours and later became one of the most valuable literary items on the Soviet black market. This fact is surprising since *The Master and Margarita* is a complex and difficult work that uses many unorthodox formal devices and thus appears to be more suitable for the reading of critics and sophisticated intelligentsia. It is therefore justified to assume that the phantasmagoric world of Bulgakov's novel appeals to mass readership since it articulates the subtext rich with allusions to the dark side of the proto-Slavic mythopoetic heritage that has remained dormant within the sphere of popular culture after the installation of the monological imperatives of the Ždanovian aesthetics.

The novel is structured around the juxtaposition of two basic narrative lines. One is devoted to the Master's novel about Christ and Pilate, the other to the adventures of the demonic Woland and his retinue in Moscow. Rita Giuliani has pointed out that this dualistic narrative structure replicates the techniques of the Ukrainian popular puppet theater called *vertep*.[1] In this form of puppet theater, the stage consists of a box with two drawers placed on top of each another, facing the audience. The theatrical action is strictly divided in *vertep* performance: the upper scene is reserved for the performance of scenes from the life of Christ while the lower is used exclusively for the intermediary sketches with comical and mundane themes in which the devil sometimes plays the leading role.

It is not difficult to recognize the structural similarity between *vertep* and the composition of *The Master and Margarita*. On the "upper scene" of the novel, the author's interpretation of Christ's Passion takes place. This is the transcendental plane, where the stylized struggle between Christ and Pilate is symbolic of the struggle of the literary artist against the power of the institution. Christ, whom Bulgakov names Ieshua Ha-Notsri, is filled with the spirit of endurance, courage, and love of humanity, in spite of his imminent death. Pilate is a tired dictator, the embodiment of the emptiness of institutional power, which devours everything human and genuine because it is concerned only with the preservation of its own dominant position. In order to achieve verisimilitude, Bulgakov employs the literary language that simulates the style of the historical novel. This device creates the impression that the most improbable, mythological events, taking place two thousand years ago in Jerusalem, appear more real than the events in contemporary Moscow. By placing the Jerusalem story on the "upper scene" and the Moscow one on the "lower," Bulgakov suggests that events of monumental importance are happening simultaneously in both places. The time frame of the novel is vastly expanded by means of this juxtaposition: it spans from the beginning of Christianity in Jerusalem to the abolition of Christianity in Moscow after the revolution.

Bulgakov treats the events in his contemporary setting as something that belongs to the "lower scene" of the novel. He introduces the Moscow of greedy apartment managers, petty criminals, and stupid literary *apparatchiks*. The language used in the Moscow episodes is much more colloquial than the language used in the Master's novel. The narrator does not emulate the voice of history and truth, but uses common urban speech. This gives the reader a sense of everyday Moscow, where people live in uncertainty, as against the "higher plane" of the novel ruled by absolute values. Bulgakov manages to employ both realistic and avant-garde novelistic poetics by positing these two distinct storylines and placing them in an implicit dialogue with each other. This quality in Bulgakov's work is characteristic of the Russian avant-garde, which wished to problematize the concept of high culture by invoking the ancient Slavic heritage preserved among the illiterate masses.[2] By drawing from the reservoir of popular culture, the artists of the avant-garde engaged the previously repressed, dark side of the Slavic mythopoetic heritage.

The "lower scene" of the novel is ruled by Woland, the dark prince of the material world, who is the parodic embodiment of the new society and its ideology. It is not accidental that Woland, like Marx, is a German who comes to haunt the Muscovites with his magical manipulations of history and reality. In the beginning of the novel, Woland has descended from the transcendental into the mundane plane to serve as the tool of the "higher" justice and punish those who are mesmerized by his power, the power of material wealth. He is closely associated with the world of popular theater and actually introduces himself to Berlioz and Bezdomny as a "specialist in black magic" at the beginning of the novel. (*MM*, 19).[3] Bulgakov, here, invokes a common medieval prejudice, which considered everyone associated with theater as a member of the diabolical tribe. It is not accidental that the devil in medieval Russia was usually referred to as the black comedian, as a figure whose actions provoked laughter as well as horror. This horrible, diabolical laughter is the first warning sign that a culture has lost its power of identification with official ideals and is sinking into a distorting cynicism. The culture that subverts its own ideals through diabolical laughter does so in order to preserve the individual identity of subjects. Woland, an obviously theatrical figure, functions as a *deus ex machina* who empowers Margarita to liberate the insane Master from the collective delusion of the official ideology of materialism.

The Master and Margarita is a novel that counters the monological vision of socialist realism by exploring the phantasmagoric world posited beyond the limits of the immediately perceivable, material reality. Bulgakov uses Christian mythology (especially its more anarchic, gnostic variants) to extend the refutation of the rationalist formula that Dostoyevski's Underground Man has initiated in the nineteenth century. Both the Master and the Underground Man are bitter and disappointed individuals, unable to identify with the dominant ideological doctrines of their age. But, while Dostoyevski's anti-hero remains forever suspended in the existentialist dilemma that does not allow him to make a choice between life of "cheap happiness" or of "lofty suffering," Bulgakov's Master is ready to choose the parodic version of "cheap happiness." He accepts all the stereotypes of romanticism at the end of the novel, affirming the transcendental value of his own writing. Both antiheros belong to the realm of subculture, but Bulgakov's Master is forced to learn the art of denial, sublimation, and parody in order to preserve his freedom and individuality and to rise above the vulgar materialism around him through artistic dissimulation. The Master's ability to rise from the depths of abjection is born exactly in the moment when he abandons the laws of the external, material world and accepts the imaginary guidance of Woland and his demons. While the Underground Man remains ambiguous in his dark corner and nurtures his twisted daydreams, the Master manages to deny the external reality of the mental hospital and to accept the imaginary world of his novel as the only valid experience. This capacity of the Master is one of the most important qualities of the borderline poetics—the world of literary representation is given a priority over a world that is being represented.

the end of mastery

The facility with which Bulgakov develops the narrative has an almost machine-like quality—the destinies of the characters are decided in accordance with the rules of already existing artistic genres. The reader does not encounter the Master, the title protagonist of the novel, until chapter thirteen, entitled "Enter the Hero." While the titles of the other chapters are related to the novelistic narrative, this one refers directly back to the process of writing. "The Hero" is treated like an actor who enters upon the stage of the novel in order to play the part reserved for him by the literary convention of the novelistic genre. Also, by giving the main protagonist the title of Master, the one who presumably possesses a superior knowledge of the literary arts, Bulgakov enhances the parodic aspect of the novel. The Master is represented as a performer who enters the stage of the literary genre to act out the ultimate identification with the world of representations.

The reader first learns of the Master as a patient in Dr. Stravinsky's mental hospital. The hero of Bulgakov's novel is miserable and depressed, in contrast with the idealized heros of socialist labor, dominant during this period of Soviet literature. But, when Ivan Bezdomny, one of the principal victims of Woland's invasion, asks him if he is a writer, he answers, somewhat offended, "I am a Master" (*MM*, 136). The Master at first appears as the embodiment of the holy fool: in order to prove his mastery to Ivan Bezdomny he puts on a black skullcap with the golden letter M embroidered on the front, thereby mocking a society where titles, ranks, and signs have become more important then essences and substantial qualities. The Master's behavior, which is in sharp contrast with the mystical knowledge he obtains through the writing of his novel about Pontius Pilate, is a stylization of the medieval Russian tradition of the holy fool, who exposes the moral shortcomings of the audience (readers in this case) by embodying them. The Master's foolishness is legitimated by his writing of a novel dealing with the confrontation between Christ and Pilate. The Master appears to be a selfish, depressed, and bitter man who cannot even remember the name of his first wife. (*MM*, 140–41) But his yearning for the truth about Christ and Pilate makes up for all his other faults.

It is precisely the Master's marginality and his desire to transcend the limits of the mundane environment that serve as a focus of Margarita's love and devotion, even though her husband, a well-established Soviet citizen, offers her ideal material conditions. Thus, Bulgakov uses the powerful mythical and psychological appeal of the romantic cliché of the seeker-in-love and her beloved. In fact, most of the critics have accepted this "romantic reading" of the novel as almost normative in studying *The Master and Margarita*.[4] But, at the same time, Bulgakov is aware that both the Master and Margarita are products of the romantic literary tradition, so he is also able to poke fun at the primeval couple. It is here that the Master comes closest to Bulgakov himself, whose literary career sharply declined after the victory of socialist realism. Laughing at the horrifying consequences of one's failure is also a sign of a healing cynicism. For Bulgakov, the only way out of the depression that the Master suffers after the attacks of the critics Latunsky and Ariman on his Biblical novel is to assume an ironic distance toward his madness and suffering. This is one of the qualities of borderline poetics: turning the experiential core of intense pain and suffering inside out and transforming it into a literary work where horror becomes laughable. This process enables the writer to distance himself from his own experience, to deny both the political reality that has caused the experience and the experience itself, and to transform that experience into a grotesque world where laughter and fear exist side by side in unresolvable tension. The letter M on the Master's cap is funny exactly because the Master is incarcerated in a mental hospital. The reader laughs because this lunatic is obviously not capable of being a master. But, at the same time, the letter M on the cap is a sign of sympathy with the struggle of the iconoclast who does not believe in the institutional way of establishing "higher" truths and chooses the path of "originality." Although this type of originality has led the Master to the mental hospital, the reader sympathizes with him because his desire to write the novel about Pilate is motivated by the romantic ideals of truth, goodness, and beauty.

The Master is a total antipode to the typical socialist realist hero. His path toward the transcendental realm cannot be identified with the prescribed struggle of the socialist toiler to overcome the constraints of the old corrupt bourgeois reality and reach the mythical realm of equality and brotherhood of all people, posited in the future by the Communist ideology. On the contrary, the Master seeks knowledge in the realm of the past by rewriting the Biblical narrative. He is a historian who works in a museum and translates from five languages. This kind of erudition makes him immediately suspect in the extreme anti-intellectual climate of the Stalinist era. The Master represents the old, pre-revolutionary intelligentsia, reminiscent of the "superfluous men" in Turgenev's novels. His erudition has in fact become so superfluous after the victory of materialism that the new Soviet society has no alternative but to confine him to an institution for the mentally ill. The Master's historical novel, based on the Biblical legend, is actually regarded as a form of madness, a useless intellectual exercise in the period of the revolutionary renewal of society. But by placing the Master in such a marginal position, Bulgakov actually wants to emphasize the fact that historical truth is often on the side of those who are excluded from the realm of "normality."

The confrontation between Christ and Pilate in the Master's rewriting of the Biblical story is presented by Bulgakov as a type of universal historical pattern whereby the individual who completely embodies the values of humanism encounters the institutionalized forms of power that are anti-humanist by definition. Pilate, who represents the anonymous and empty institution of the Roman law in Jerusalem, is confronted by a Christ figure who dares to deny almost every principle on which that law is based. Bulgakov uses a similar pattern of confrontation throughout *The Master and Margarita*, especially in the encounters of Ivan Bezdomny and Dr. Stravinsky in the mental hospital and during the Master's struggle with the official literary critics. There is a point in the novel in which Bulgakov subtly lays bare the use of this device. When, during their first conversation in the mental hospital, the Master asks his fellow patient Ivan Bezdomny why he was committed, the latter replies: "Because of Pontius Pilate" (*MM*, 135), alluding to the fact that everyone on a quest, independent of the instituted sense of "reality," is bound to encounter a Pilate-like figure who will restore the pre-established order by marginalizing the one who dares to question and resist it. And, although each individual who starts to follow the path of resistance is physically or mentally destroyed on the "lower stage" of the novel, each also receives a reward from the "upper stage" where the laws of material existence are transcended. Even though most of the characters on this path lack Christ's courage, love, and compassion, they are nevertheless distinguished from simple mortals. The Master is the best example of how *imitatio Christi* fails when there is not enough spiritual courage to persist in the personal struggle against an institutionalized ideology.

Bulgakov's hero does not possess the ability of the socialist realist hero to pick himself up and continue the righteous struggle against the remains of the old and corrupt society. This capacity was appropriated by Communist ideology from Christianity and transformed into a specific novelistic form of propaganda. The socialist realist hero possesses a complete faith in the Communist ideals and is therefore rewarded for his struggle. Instead of God, the reward comes from the factory manager, the Party commissar, or even Stalin himself. The realm of high religious values is now brought down to the material, earthly level where the same religious struggle of dark and light divinities is acted out under a different set of masks. In fact, what was material and low in Christian ideology becomes ideal and high in the Communist one. This idealization of the material is in fact the target of Bulgakov's satirical stance against the greedy Muscovites who lie, steal, and denounce one another in order to accumulate more material wealth.

But the Master is not willing to fit into such social context. He gives up trying to publish his novel about Pilate and withdraws from this reality of corruption. His moods fluctuate between depression and amazement, until finally he becomes fearful and burns the manuscript of his novel. The Master's fear and cowardice are signs of his ultimate failure in the struggle against the literary institution, but they are also a necessary condition for his transition to the transcendental realm. His relationship with Margarita does not save him from a mental crisis at this point in the novel. Her love is only secondary to his desire to publish a novel and be accepted as a writer. The Master experiences a nervous breakdown and, sitting by the fire, whispers: "Something terrible has happened to me . . . Come, come, please come . . . !" (*MM*, 146). The Master is alone in the room, and it is not clear at first whom he is inviting to come. Margarita arrives too late in his basement apartment to stop him from burning the manuscript. She is able to save only a part of it and leaves, promising to get a divorce, to return the next day, and to stay with the Master forever. But "a quarter of an hour after she had left me there came a knock at my window . . . " (*MM*, 148) says the excited Master, recounting the whole story to Ivan Bezdomny, who is able to hear only these introductory words. Ivan is not able to understand who else besides Margarita visits the apartment, because the noises in the mental hospital corridor constantly interfere with the Master's story. The reader learns only those things that Ivan is able to catch during their interrupted conversation. "Now and again a spasm would cross his [the Master's] face. Fear and anger sparkled in his eyes. The narrator pointed in the direction of the moon, which had long since disappeared from the balcony." (*MM*, 148). Bulgakov deliberately drowns the Master's voice in the "noise" of the hospital corridor in order to obscure the true identity of the mysterious visitor. But the Master's call for help and the full moon are clear allusions to the Faustian subtext of the novel. When all the other means of recovery from depression fail, the Master tries to get help from the "other," darker world. And since he is not ready yet to understand the nature of the power that responds to his call, his fear grows into panic and he ends up committing himself to the mental hospital. The failure of the Master's courage is completed by this act of passive submission to the institutional power. He gives up his poetic search for the truth about Christ and Pilate and vows never to write again. His failure is a symptom of the collapse of the entire tradition of the "great Russian novel" during the Soviet era.

After the Master's incarceration, the novelistic action is perceived simultaneously from two opposing perspectives. From the mundane "lower scene," the fantastic events in the novel appear to be the product of the imagination of the crazed Master. But from the perspective of the "upper scene," these events are a revelation of the ultimate, transcendental reality. There is, thus, a tension between the two possible readings, so that the "true" meaning and value of the Master's art remain indeterminable. In the context of a materialistically minded Moscow, the Master is seen as a social misfit whose literary messages about Christ and Pilate are dated and dangerous for the new revolutionary system. Therefore, on this "lower" plane of the narrative, the only fit place for his ideas is the asylum where his "madness" may be successfully contained and transformed into "mental disease." On the other hand, Margarita's love for the Master turns his novel into a vehicle of higher knowledge that enables the lovers to transcend the mundane and reach the "upper stage" of novelistic action. This other, supernatural register of the novel is saturated with fantasies that are characteristic of wish fulfillment. Woland, who descends upon Moscow as a tool of this higher justice, is almost certainly one of Bulgakov's compensatory projections. All the aggressive energies that Bulgakov had to repress and hide during the campaign against him are now channeled through Woland. Most of the characters from the "lower world" are punished for their material greed, small-mindedness, and corruption by Woland and his demons.

From this higher point of view, the Master resembles a gnostic who learns about the basic principles of transcendental reality by writing his novel. His search is completely iconoclastic, and that makes him extremely vulnerable and confused. The Master loses all confidence in his novel about Pilate and, while in the mental hospital, accepts the "lower stage" perspective and his own madness. When he is elevated from the hospital to the upper plane of the novel, he reveals his true feelings to Woland: "I hate that novel. I have been through too much because of it" (*MM*, 286). Bulgakov condemns this attitude as a sign of moral weakness that prevents the Master from achieving "light" at the end of the novel. The nature of the Master's achievement is revealed to the reader through the statement of the "real" author of the Gospel, Matthew the Levite: "He [Christ] has read the Master's writings and asks you [Woland] to take the Master with you and reward him by granting him peace." (*MM*, 349). Thus, Christ himself is validating the Master's version, implying that it is closer to the "truth" about his crucifixion than the official version of Matthew.

The problem of truthfulness is complicated by the narrative structure of the novel. The reader learns about Christ's words either from the Master's novel or from the story Woland tells Berlioz and Bezdomny at the beginning of the novel. When questioned by Pilate about Matthew's version of Biblical events, Christ says: "But I once caught a glimpse of that parchment and I was horrified. I had not said a word of what was written there" (*MM*, 25). Is not Christ denying the validity of Matthew's gospel in favor of the Master's apocryphal version of the Passion story? But at the same time, is Woland, the devil, capable of speaking the truth? Or, even if he does speak the truth, is not that truth again a lie precisely because it is spoken by the devil? And, by the same logic, is not the Master's novel, which is placed in the same narrative sequence as Woland's story, just an apocryphal interpretation of Christ's destiny and not "the truth?" At this point, the novel starts to resist simplistic "yes or no" interpretations. According to Linda Hutcheon, the problematization of borders between the literary and the extra-literary and the questioning of totalizing systems of representation is characteristic of postmodernism.[5] The novelistic continuum is exploded into a multitude of alternating realities that are all equally truthful and illusory at the same time. In a conversation with Ivan Bezdomny, the Master implies that there is a way of understanding the world that goes beyond disjunctive logic: "Both you and I are mad, there's no point in denying it. He [Woland] gave you a shock and it sent you mad, because you were temperamentally liable to react that way. Nevertheless what you have described unquestionably happened in fact. . . . The man you were talking to [Woland] *was* with Pontius Pilate, he did have breakfast with Kant and now he has paid a call on Moscow" (*MM*, 137).

Bulgakov is trying to convey the idea that the Master's madness is not to be regarded as a delusion, but as an original epistemological mode bringing superior insight. The Master, like a contemporary holy fool, is able to gain superior knowledge by revelation that comes from the "upper stage" of the world order. Because of his contact with the higher world, he is encapsulated in an aura of holiness, the surface of which is truthful and funny at the same time. But the Master's holiness is not of the absolute kind because he has succumbed to the pressures of the new atheistic society. His reward in the other world comes from Woland and not from Christ. In the chapter entitled "The Fate of the Master and Margarita is Decided" that takes place on the "upper" scene of the novelistic stage, Woland asks Matthew the Levite: "Why don't you take him yourself to the side of light?" (*MM*, 349). Woland, the ruler of the dark, material side of existence, thinks that the Master should be granted eternal light because he had guessed the "truth" about Christ and Pilate. "'He has not earned light, he has earned rest,' said the Levite sadly" (*MM*, 349). It is interesting that *pokoy*, the Russian word for rest, or even better, peace, has definite resonances of death, since the derived word *pokoynik* denotes the deceased one. So the only reward that the Master gets for writing his novel is the state of peaceful nonbeing that he will be granted after death. But why does not the Master qualify for the obviously higher prize of light?

In the first place, the Master did not turn to light when he was cornered by the literary critics. Instead, he sank deeper into depression and ended up invoking the powers of darkness. The knock on his window was a sign that those powers were invading his life, and that the invasion was going to continue with Woland's visit to Moscow. Indirectly, the Master causes this demonic invasion, because he and Margarita are the only ones who benefit from the havoc Woland creates in Moscow. Margarita's transformation into a witch, triggered by her pact with Woland, is a tool that is used by the powers of darkness to punish those who had destroyed the Master's literary reputation. So, instead of seeking help from Christ, whom he uses only as a secondary character in his novel, the Master loses faith and accepts help from the dark side. He is not strong enough to travel the path of a saint whose holiness is based on the best human qualities. He abandons his struggle and becomes self-destructive. The Master actually feels so low on the scale of humanity that he gives up his name. "I no longer have a name. I have renounced it. Let us forget about it" (*MM*, 138).

The Master's proper name is replaced by the parodic sign of his mastery. This lack of a proper name indicates a loss of personal essence or of a soul, which the Master has had to renounce once he has immersed himself in the practice of writing and invoked the powers of darkness. Every writing that is not sanctioned directly by the official ideology or religion is implicitly heretical and associated with the forbidden side of reality. His self-proclaimed mastery is used parodically in reference to the Russian literary tradition of imaginative writing. This tradition, which originated in the Neoplatonic ideals of Russian romanticism and reached its culmination in the works of Gogol, Dostoyevski, Byeli, and Sologub, was completely negated during the socialist realist period of Russian literature. The transcendental yearning for metaphysical knowledge of the world beyond the material was transformed in the Soviet era into a revolutionary fervor to turn the old and corrupt world into an earthly paradise. The imaginative literature that exploited religious, mythological, and magical themes was scorned as a useless bourgeois pastime that could not rival the socialist realist literature of the new materialist empire.

The Master is a casualty of this new pragmatism because his writing extends beyond the limits of the self-evident reality and reaches for the immutable, transcendental world, represented in the novel by the Christian myth of Christ and Pilate. His imagination refuses to be subjugated by the concrete ideological circumstances of his era. But, since the world of Soviet atheism does not accept such an irrationalist credo, the Master is forced to withdraw to the "upper stage" where he can commence his eternal existence among the literary characters who take part in his novel. The living man, thus, is so absorbed by his own writing that he becomes a character in his own novel. This transformation from mad writer into a literary Master is performed by Bulgakov in a manner that is parodic and straightforward at the same time. At the very end of the Master's and Margarita's journey to the "upper stage" of being, Woland reveals what is the ultimate destiny of the Master: "Oh, thrice Romantic master, wouldn't you like to stroll under the cherry blossoms with your love in the daytime and listen to Schubert in the evening? Won't you enjoy writing by candlelight with a goose quill? Don't you want, like Faust, to sit over a retort in the hope of fashioning a new homunculus? That's where you must go—where a house and an old servant are already waiting for you and the candles are lit—although they are soon to be put out because you will arrive at dawn. That is your way, Master, that way!" (*MM*, 371).

The imaginary landscape described by Woland is the idealized setting that will accommodate the "thrice Romantic master" and his beloved Margarita when they enter the fantastic dimension of their literary afterlife. By placing the Master and Margarita in an environment derived from the literary commonplaces of the romantic tradition, Bulgakov defines his archetypal lovers as the artefacts that are produced and contained by the literary tradition itself. The age of literary mastery inspired by metaphysical and transcendental longings is being systematically replaced by the literary engineering that consciously serves the dominant materialist ideology. Bulgakov's Master is the last, unrecognized romantic seeker, standing at the end of this literary tradition. The place of his eternal refuge is filled with romantic stereotypes. Woland's speech to the Master is spiced with irony, implicit in his reference to Faust as the ideal romantic man. The intertextual relationship with Faust turns the Master into a seeker after truth who, like a true literary alchemist, hopes to create "a new homunculus" and overcome the boundaries imposed on him by the Philistines of his age.

The end of Bulgakov's Master is the end of the great Russian tradition of imaginative literature, a tradition free from the constraints of the socialist realist demand for the "authentic, historically specific depiction of reality in its revolutionary development."[6] *The Master and Margarita* closes the cycle of writings that make use of fantastic elements in order to touch on the metaphysical questions that were vital to the Russian novelists of the nineteenth century, to the twentieth-century Symbolists, and to some members of the Russian avant-garde. Imaginative writing was left behind in the 1930s because it absorbed literary talents that were needed for the socialist reconstruction of the Russian cultural heritage.

gnosis and death

The dual model of early Slavic culture reveals that the oppositions between certain aspects of social, political, and cultural structures were constructed from the initial opposition between Chernobog and Byelobog, predating the Christian period of Slavic culture. During the Middle Ages this initial opposition was transformed into the struggle between the worlds of Satan and Christ. Bulgakov employs the same principle to organize the novelistic material of *The Master and Margarita*, juxtaposing events in contemporary Moscow, which cannot resist the temptations of Woland, with those in Jerusalem, which are the subject of the Master's novel. The desire of the Master to understand and describe the transcendental dimension of Christ's suffering and death is opposed by the corrupt world of the Moscow writers, who sacrifice their artistic integrity to improve their social and material status. The Master appears to be the only writer above such petty material considerations. For the other writers in *The Master and Margarita*, writing is only the necessary evil that gains them entry into a Writer's Union restaurant and enables them to have free room and board in one of the Union's dachas on the seacoast. The Master's interest in the universe beyond the material one and his deep scorn for the world of matter are rooted in an older division that was already evident within early Christianity. This sharp opposition between the mundane and the transcendental is characteristic of a number of gnostic sects, whose teachings remained influential in eastern and southern Slavic regions long after their disappearance in the West.

An interest in gnosticism was characteristic of Russian literature as a whole at the turn of the century. Bulgakov's own interest in the occult sciences had a number of precedents in the works of the Symbolists, who believed that the writer, like Bulgakov's Master, mediates between the hidden world of absolutes and the manifest world of relative existence. The opposition between these two structural elements originates in the teachings of the Christian gnostics, who believed that the universe is divided into the absolutely sinful material world, created by the demiurge, and the transcendental world, based on truth and virtue, which is concealed within the first one. Knowledge of the latter dimension is the aim of *gnosis*, of the mystical insight that is supposed to abolish the split between the gnostic seeker and the true God residing in the realm beyond the material world. "The world is the alienating element between man and God. The salvation is the reestablishment of wholeness. It is a self-salvation of God through 'real knowledge' and catharsis. The real God resides completely outside of the boundaries of the physical universe. It is unknowable (*naturaliter ignotus*), unspeakable, it is a non-being (Basilides). By defining God in those terms, gnosticism becomes the source of negative (apophatic) theology and bears close resemblance to Buddhism."[7]

The material world is viewed by the gnostics as a source of illusory projections that obstruct the seeker in his spiritual journey toward God. Reality is defined in negative terms, as the source of sin and deception that lure the seeker away from the unity that he wishes to establish with the invisible world of God. Unlike the "official" Christian God who is defined by his omnipresence, the gnostic God is defined by his absence from the material world. The gnostics strongly rejected the material wealth of the official church and viewed the mundane world as a place dominated by a superfluity of sound and fury.

The Master's disgust with the citizens of Moscow, whose lack of understanding forces him to commit himself to the mental hospital, exemplifies this gnostic attitude. During the hospital encounter with

Ivan Bezdomny, the Master declares: "You see, I can't bear noise, disturbance, violence or anything of that sort. I particularly hate the sound of people screaming, whether it is the scream of pain, anger, or any other kind of scream" (*MM*, 134). The Master displays an elitist scorn for the people and their violent emotions, which are somehow not noble enough for his artistic ears. The desire for silence, for the nonconflictual state of unity with the transcendental God, is a disguised expression of the death drive. When all sounds die down, when the body becomes still like a corpse, then the world of the spirit emerges. The necessary condition for the emergence of this "higher reality" is the death of the body and the end of life in the mundane reality.

According to gnostic teachings, "death liberates the soul, while the body is its grave or a dungeon inside which the soul is imprisoned."[8] The gnostic can achieve his aim only after a radical denial of the body and the life drive has been enacted. This unconscious element is embedded in Bulgakov's novelistic plan; the Master craves peace that is possible only after he and Margarita are poisoned and then resurrected by Azazello, who then leads them into the transcendental realm which is built out of romantic clichés. As soon as they are reborn in the "upper" world, the Master has a revelation:

> "Ah, I understand," said the Master, gazing around, "you have killed us. We are dead. How clever and how timely! Now I see it all."
>
> "Oh, come," replied Azazello, "what did I hear you say? Your beloved calls you the Master, you're an intelligent being—how can you be dead? It's ridiculous."
>
> "I understand what you mean," cried the Master, "don't go on! You are right—a thousand times right!" (*MM*, 359)

The convergence of the two narrative lines at the end of *The Master and Margarita* indicates that the heroes have reached the state of peaceful nonbeing (*pokoy*), which was the supreme aim of the gnostics. Bulgakov does not let us know what the Master understands, but he hints at a belief that true life starts after the seeker is released from the fetters of existence in the material world. Gnostics believed in the ascent of the soul, which achieves the plenitude of being in the transcendental dimension after death. The Master is able to reach complete understanding or *gnosis* only after death, which liberates him from the confinement of the materialistic life of Moscow and, more literally, from the boundaries of Dr. Stravinsky's asylum. According to Kurt Rudolph, the release of the soul is the final step in the achievement of *gnosis*. "The redemption guaranteed by means of 'knowledge', in the sense of an escape from the entanglements of earthly existence, is first realized by the gnostic at the time of his death, for at this moment he encounters the everlasting, reawakening fact of release from the fetters of the body, and is able to set out on the way to his true home."[9]

Only two years before its author's death in 1940, Bulgakov's novel turned into a type of gnostic gospel, which helped him to "rise above" his own incurable illness and the hostile critical reactions to his work. He was able to enjoy the provisional comfort offered by the process of writing, which transformed his agony into a work of art that would survive his physical death. Since he could no longer find an outlet for his ideas in the external world of institutional literature and theater, Bulgakov turned completely inward, toward the space of imagination where autobiographical phantasies could be acted out on both the "lower" and "upper" scene at the same time. The literary critics are punished by Woland, the Master and Margarita are reunited in the afterlife, and Jesus forgives Pilate his sin of inner cowardice. The escapist solution at the end of the novel is motivated by the transference of Bulgakov's experience of rejection by the new Soviet society into the narrative drama of *The Master and Margarita*. This transformation of the prose into an artefact which is more real then the external reality is typical of borderline poetics, guaranteeing imaginary satisfaction while it sublimates the external causes of one's suffering. Literature literally becomes more real then reality, because the borderline author divests the world of external circumstances and invests language with a horrifying power of obliteration.

At the time that he was secretly dictating the final draft of the novel in 1938, Bulgakov wrote to his third wife Yelena Sergeyevna about an article on the fantastic tales of E. T. A. Hoffmann, which assured him that he was on the right track with *The Master and Margarita*. The article in question, authored by Mirimsky, states that "the artist rises at will above all that is finite, including his own art. In the incorporeal realm which he creates, the artist's will can be regarded as a universal tool of liberation from the real world." [10] The gnostic rejection of the "real world," which is achieved by the implementation of the "artist's will," reveals Bulgakov's motivation in practicing an art which will offer a refuge through the magical production of signs. This magical operation uses the linguistic sign as a shield against hostile reality and transforms reality into a sign of happy forgetfulness. At the same time, this magical production of signs confronts the reader with the agony of the individual struggling for identity, which is erased by the massive collectivization of consciousness in the Soviet society of the 1930s. The salvation and redemption of both the Master and his creator are found in the artistic process itself, in the promise inherent in the act of writing, which grants the promise of reaching beyond the present, material world of suffering and of finding the "way to true home."

Bulgakov was persistent in applying the principles of this "passive" side of the romantic tradition while rejecting the Soviet ideological program of "revolutionary romanticism," which did not allow the individual to find alternatives to the doctrines posited by the Party.[11] Trotsky's proclamation that the word is only the phonetic shadow of the deed was a definite blow to the claims of the avant-garde theorists who, like Bulgakov, advocated the theory of the autonomous power of the word. Like a high church official, Trotsky had to defend the monolithic position of the Party, whose "deeds" are beyond questioning and whose programs can only be followed. Literature and art could not construct the future on the principles of the engaged but autonomous artistic imagination, but had to reflect what the Party imagined and decided. The Party ideology was officially dialectical materialism, but that materialism was as imaginary as any reality constituted by means of written documents. The dialectics evolved between the Party which dictated and the people who reacted. Literature was to channel those reactions, to educate the illiterate masses and instill high Party ideals in the manner of the canonized Gospels.

Gnosticism was the first alternative movement within Christianity which developed its own rites and scriptures, unmediated by the rigid hierarchy of the official church. Its followers were persecuted for their heretical teachings, which had many analogies with the pre-Christian cosmogonies. They were the first to recognize the dark, residual element of paganism which the official church had sublimated through Christ's sacrifice. Some gnostic sects preached the dual nature of God and worshiped the body as the dark element which is used as a vessel for the achievement of the light one. They also believed in the primacy of the word over faith. The opening of the Gospel of St. John, "In the beginning was the word (*logos*)," was most frequently referred to by the gnostics, who believed in the redemptive function of the word. The soul was sick, lived in the house of poverty (i.e., the body), and hungered for the word to "lay it like a medicament upon its eyes that it may see (again), and its light hide the enemies who strive with it, and it may blind them with the light . . ." [12]

The sickness of the soul is recognized as an important element in the journey toward the light which is accomplished through the implementation of the word. Like the mad Master, who dies to get rid of his sick soul and to ride with the characters of his own invention on the transcendental plain, the gnostic strives after the word which brings enlightenment and salvation. The Master reaches the "upper" scene by using the novelistic word, which necessarily falsifies the truth posited in the official Gospels. He changes the name of Jesus to Ieshua Ha-Notsri, in order to get away from the mythologized image of Jesus presented in the Holy Writ. This strategic move provides access to a "living Christ," a gnostic formula for the ordinary nature of Jesus. In characteristically dualistic fashion, the gnostics believed that besides the transient from Nazareth, there is another figure of a "heavenly Christ" who serves as the liberator of the soul. Both of these figures appear in *The Master and Margarita*, the first as the de-mythologized Ieshua Ha-Notsri in the Master's novel, while the second is used in the framing narrative. This other, spiritual emanation of Christ in the Jerusalem narrative is usually referred to only as "he" or the man whom Pilate "longs to join" (*MM*, 370). The figure of Christ is never represented outside the Master's novel. The Christ which belongs to the "upper scene" of the novel is

only spoken of by Woland and Matthew the Levite. This second,
invisible emanation of Christ, which liberates Pilate from the injustice he has done in yielding to the pressure of Kaiafas, asks Woland to provide the Master and Margarita with their eternal refuge. The narrative harmony initiated by Bulgakov at the beginning of the novel is later disturbed by the diabolical pranks of Woland and his demons on the "lower scene."

The relationship between Jesus and Woland in the novel is indeed reminiscent of the relationship between the gnostic transcendental god, accessible to the few, and the demiurge, the creator of the material world. Woland rules over the masses, bent on the acquisition and accumulation of material goods, and embodies a parody of Stalinist vulgar materialism. Junker Woland, one of Faust's incarnations, comes under a guise of the German professor of black magic to enlighten the Muscovites about the nature of material wealth. He turns rubles into foreign currency, causes illness, and practices mass hypnosis. Margarita is the first mortal who is enlisted by Woland. She is not able to communicate directly with the realm of light, but first has to deal with the powers of the material world. She is ordered by Azazello, the killing demon, to rub her body with a magical cream which makes her invisible and helps her fly through the air. She is then introduced to Woland, who turns her into a hostess at the Satanic ball which takes place in the "fifth dimension." After the ball, Margarita finds Woland playing chess with the demonic cat Behemoth. Hella, the female vampire, is massaging Woland's knee with a steaming ointment. "Near Woland was a strange globe, lit from one side, which seemed almost alive" (*MM*, 250). In the circus-like atmosphere of comic terror, the reader learns that the globe is a kind of prototelevision screen. It enables Woland to see everything that is happening in the material world.

The satanic nature of Woland originates in the gnostic, especially Bogumil, elaboration of the Christian myth. According to the Bogumils, the name of the creator of this world was Satanael, changed to Satan only after his fall from the grace of the invisible god.[13] Bulgakov's Woland is the incarnation of this powerful spirit, which is oriented toward evil actions in the name of the supreme good. The Master and Margarita are the last righteous inhabitants of Moscow who are able to use Woland as an ally, since they manage to overcome the power of the material world through their longing for the transcendental one. Margarita's love and the Master's art are the tools for obtaining the help of the devil, who, being ultimately the agent of the invisible god, leads them into the realm of eternal silence.

The Bogumils also rejected the world created by Satanael and regarded the official, material church and its sacraments and icons as a political power which was on its way to becoming as corrupt as the secular institution of the state. Bulgakov's attitude to the new revolutionary state was very similar, since he despised the material revolution and its effects and affirmed romantic salvation through art and love. Woland comes to demonstrate his magical powers and show the shortcomings of the dominant ideology of dialectical materialism which is now constructed by the new, human entities. From Lenin to Stalin, Party ideology stresses the construction of the "new reality," which replaces Christian mythology with the Soviet perversion of Marxist theories. The power which once belonged to God and Emperor is gathered suddenly in the hands of one man who is able to mobilize and lead the masses. The old hierarchy is replaced by the new one, with the pretension of reviving the revolutionary ideals of freedom, brotherhood, and equality. Under the guise of revolution, the instrumental ethic of horror forces every individual to participate in the building of the new empire. The old Christian ideology is only apparently erased, since individual salvation in Soviet society continued to depend on the "world beyond" the immediate present. The Communist dream posits its ideals in the future classless society whose popular ideological formulations have definite paradisiacal overtones. Woland counters this idealistic proposition and shows the transitory nature of human life based entirely on existence in the material realm. This marginal, gnostic relationship toward any official ideology is the foundation of Bulgakov's borderline poetics in *The Master and Margarita*.

Gnostic insistence on the transitory nature of the material world increases usually when a society enters a state of deep political crisis. The word, the divine logos, becomes more real than the world of bodies and things. The insistence of the Russian avant-gardists on *samovitoe slovo*, on the autonomous nature of the word, which is itself the source of the poetic drive, is certainly a symptom of such a climate. The word is resurrected and freed from the constraints of referentiality in the prerevolutionary literary movements and remains free until first Trotsky and then Ždanov pinned it down with a demand for realism. This is the moment when the word loses its autonomy and is treated only as a reflection of a concrete social and political order. The first period of the Russian Revolution was such a time, the gnostic divine logos being incarnated in the semiotic outbursts of the futurists. The latter simulated the actual revolution in poetic terms. The assimilation of Marxist ideas in Russia had a similar effect on the mass ideology of communism, which used the discourse of liberation in order to further enslave the masses of impoverished peasants. Jerotić claims that Russian Marxism was blended with ancient gnostic and apocalyptic traditions.

> Russian Marxism, by using such terminology as dialectics and alienation, shows that it has its roots not only in the British economic thought, French social practice and materialist science, but also in the neoplatonic, gnostic, eschatological and apocalyptic traditions in Russia (via Byzantium). . . . The liberation of mankind, the abolishment of the state, the transitional period of dictatorship in the Marxist vision of the historical process has its roots in the gnostic and apocalyptic teachings about salvation. Marxism never managed to detach itself from those mythic and utopian roots, and similarly to the Christianity in the medieval period, quickly transformed itself into Scholasticism.[14]

Socialist realism was imposing its scholastic requirements at the time Bulgakov was writing *The Master and Margarita*. The great utopian potential that the Russian revolution had for liberating the word from oppressive exploitation by the "powers of this world" quickly turned into an unprecedented terror of the word. Anyone whose interests and concerns were not those of the new materialist ideology was labeled a fossilized remnant of the past who did not deserve a place in the new world. The gnostic concept of freedom, as the boundless expansion into the potential space beyond an immediately perceivable reality, was quickly transformed into a dogmatic vision of constraints based upon the dictums of material necessity.

mikhail bulgakov

The determinist concept of freedom, borrowed by the Soviet ideologists from Engels, forced the individual to submit to the necessities proclaimed by the official Party platform, necessities which were presented as the objective reality. By the end of the 1930s, the utopian space of the classless society has gained the same axiological status as the Kingdom of Heaven in the Christian mythology, and is being used as an empty rhetorical device by ideologists. This lost utopian space, incarnated in Marxism by Bloch's *Prinzip Hoffnung*, is the dimension which Bulgakov has fictionalized in *The Master and Margarita* on the "upper scene" of novelistic action. The entire novel can be read as an attempt to save the utopian space of boundless freedom which was rapidly vanishing during the period of Stalinization. In the moment when Azazello resurrects the Master and Margarita and prepares them for the final journey to the "upper scene," they decide to burn down the remnants of their old life and get rid of everything which binds them to the earthly realm.

> "Then the fire!" cried Azazello. "The Fire—where it all began and where we shall end it!"
> "The fire!" Margarita cried in a terrible voice. . . .
> The Master, intoxicated in advance by the thought of the ride to come, threw a book from the bookcase onto the table, thrust its leaves into the burning tablecloth, and the book burst merrily into flame.
> "Burn away, past life!"
> "Burn, suffering," cried Margarita. (*MM*, 359)

By invoking the fire and burning down the "past life," the protagonists of the novel are destroying the material side of existence and preparing to enter the utopian sphere where life will unfold in accordance with their wishes. All ties to the material world are broken and their souls are purified through fire, the fundamental gnostic element, symbolizing the "divine spark," the true transformative potential present within each individual. The fire is lit only within those who are able to give up their material existence and pursue the world beyond on their own terms.

The Master and Margarita is a novel which celebrates individual salvation and scorns the massive, ideologized construction of the material world preached by the politicians. Bulgakov reacts to the extreme secularization of the mind which Soviet society underwent after the revolution. He is motivated by the struggle for the individual psychic space which cannot be completely assimilated by positivist formulas and ideological programs. This imaginary space resists ideologization because it belongs to the realm of free play and parody, to the law of absolute romantic desire, in which individualistic anarchism denies the power of institutional norms. This desire, embodied in the novel in the Master's urge to rewrite the story of Christ's Passion and in Margarita's love, is a way of defying the dictums of the mundane, average, and accepted modes of thought and behavior. Woland expresses this rebellion of the dark side in his debate with Matthew the Levite: "Think now: Where would your good be if there were no evil, and what would the world look like without shadow? Shadows are thrown by people and things. There's the shadow of my sword, for instance. But shadows are also cast by trees and living beings. Do you want to strip the whole globe by removing every tree and every creature to satisfy your fantasy of a bare world?" (*MM*, 348).

Woland identifies the "evil" with the shadow things cast, with the part of existence that resists the world organized on rational principles; the "evil" positions itself always against the dominant ideology. The shadow represents the space of the darker side of the soul, behind which borderline poetics erects its defenses against the collectivization of the human mind. The irrationalist distortion of the rationally organized world of institutional mentality is a uniquely human method for the assertion of individuality. Woland comes to Moscow to demonstrate the uncertain nature of a world based on Marxist rationality, but also to show to the Master and Margarita how all his actions are ultimately sanctioned by the power of good. The ambiguous epigram to *The Master and Margarita,* borrowed from Goethe's *Faust,* becomes clearer if we consider the gnostic subtexts of the novel: "That Power I serve/Which wills forever evil/Yet does forever good." Woland, in his earthly emanation, is the spirit who "wills evil" and rules over the material world and its corrupted institutions. If a character in the novel is too attached to material goods, he becomes the victim of Woland's evil actions. On the other hand, from the perspective of the "upper scene" of the novel, Woland's actions are good, since he hurts only those who do not recognize the transitory nature of the material world and who cause evil by their own attachments to it. The destiny of Stepa Likhodeyev, Rimsky, Varenukha, and others, who are punished by Woland because they succumb to their lower natures, displays the ruler of the material world only as a tool of higher justice, which is banished to the hidden, transcendental sphere by official atheism. Only those who practice love and art are able to reach the last refuge, with the help of Woland, the prince of darkness.

agape and sophia

Margarita enters the pact with Woland in order to find and save her beloved Master from the mental hospital. She acquires magical powers and demolishes the apartment of the literary critic Latunsky, author of a malevolent article about the Master's novel, in order to avenge the Master, who goes crazy after a series of rejections by the literary establishment. Margarita represents the side of Slavic femininity which is derived from and then opposed to the Damp Mother Earth myth. She appears on the novelistic scene as a protean female presence, a derivation of the gnostic concept of Pistis Sophia.

She is the only actively human protagonist in the novel and is sharply juxtaposed to the other characters, who are passive, one-dimensional, and puppet-like. While the Muscovites are bewitched and manipulated by Woland and his crew, behaving like puppets in a *vertep* performance, Margarita actively bargains with Azazello and of her own free will enters into a pact with the demonic forces. In contrast to the Master, who fails to assert his art and acts like a coward, Margarita possesses almost superhuman courage and energy to fight for what she desires. While the Master allows himself to sink into depression, she embodies the active principle of love, the divine Sophia, the demiurge's helpmate in the creation of the world.

Margarita's role of queen and hostess at Satan's ball becomes clearer in the light of the gnostic conception of creation. Woland, who is ruler over the material realm, needs a female companion in order to gather all the other sinners during the spring full moon. This ritual repetition of the creation story takes place at Satan's ball, where Woland and Margarita play the parodic roles of the primal couple. The gnostic conception explicitly ties the creation of the material realm to the cooperation of the demiurge with a female being who is the embodiment of wisdom and faith. "The world of the creator [demiurge] is subordinated to the world which lies in front of it in space and time, and at the same time is thereby devaluated; its origin is to be explained from a disharmony which somehow enters in at the margin of the upper world. A female being is responsible for this, who bears the name 'Wisdom' (Sophia) and 'Faith' (Pistis)—the first evidently with an eye on the figure of "Wisdom" known from the Jewish wisdom literature, who functions as the assistant to God in creation. . . ."[15]

Since Woland plays the part of the lesser god, who creates and rules the material universe, his assistant at the demonic ball has to be a female figure who, like Margarita, possesses both faith and wisdom. By means of magic, Margarita is first transformed into a witch and then into a queen at Satan's ball. She is supposed to entertain the most prominent and the most sinful group of shades, who are celebrating the dark side of existence. Margarita, the true hero of the novel, ascends into the fifth dimension beyond space and time and acts as a hostess in order to get a reward from Woland. She has to recognize her lower nature first in order to be transformed later into a principle of higher justice. Both of the ambivalent aspects of the feminine element are expressed in the gnostic poem called "Thunder, Perfect Mind," which invokes the opposites which constitute this polar projection of the feminine: "I am the first and the last" and "I am godless, and I am one whose God is great."[16] Margarita is freed from the chains of mundane existence because she recognizes and persists in her love for the Master and his art. The sense of boundless freedom expressed in the gnostic poem reflects Margarita's character, which, when liberated from the constraints of patriarchal ethics, acts in accordance with the power of her desire. She conquers fear and the weight of her body and flies through the air like a witch. After anointing herself with Azazello's cream, she becomes invisible and quite literally enters the world of bodiless spirits. "You can have everything in the room," she says ecstatically to her maid Natasha. This statement indicates that her transformation is final and irrevocable (*MM*, 228). She has no need for the material world anymore and is ready to embrace the freedom that the magical flight can offer.

From the perspective of the "lower scene," Margarita is the "fallen Sophia" whose uncontrolled passion is responsible for the misery in the material world. She makes both her husband and the Master suffer before her transformation. This "lower" aspect of Margarita's character is responsible for her adultery and her decision to leave her husband, although he is a perfect companion in the context of the material world. She also arrives too late to save the Master from his basement apartment, which is transformed into a prison after his literary defeat. Margarita awakens to her true desire only when the dark side contacts her and confirms her intuition that she has to pursue her love if she wants to avoid the misery of her idealized material existence without love. The power of love transforms her into the "incorruptible Sophia," the perfect feminine redeeming power which saves the Master from despair and helps him reach the "upper scene" of the novel. That love is *agape*, the idealized and sublimated erotic attraction between human beings, manifested as the love of God. Margarita falls in love with the Master after she finds out about his obsession with his novel about Pilate and Christ.

Margarita is really in love with the Jerusalem represented in the Master's novel and not with the Master's foolish and awkward earthly incarnation. This brings her even closer to Sophia, the emanation of wisdom which helps the independent seekers after the divine truth on their way to true knowledge. Margarita's destiny changes when she thinks the thought which is "read" by Azazello: "I'd sell my soul to the devil to know whether he's alive or not. . . " (*MM*, 220). The demon finds her as soon as she is ready to "sell her soul" in order to gain knowledge of the invisible, other world. Once she finds out that the Master is alive, she assumes the attitude of selflessness and compassion, and this enables her to have enough strength to face the devil and become the hostess at Satan's ball. Bulgakov is representing Margarita's love as the ideal human value which slowly fades when confronted with the rationalist organization of the mundane world around him. At the very beginning of the second part of the book, largely devoted to Margarita's ascent into the fifth dimension, Bulgakov addresses the reader directly:

> Follow me reader! Who told you that there is no such thing as real, true, eternal love? Cut out his lying tongue!
>
> Follow me, reader, and only me, and I will show you that love!
>
> The Master was wrong when he told Ivan with such bitterness, in the hospital that hour before midnight, that she had forgotten him. It was impossible. Of course she had not forgotten him. (*MM*, 213)

Just as in the case of the Master's quest for literary mastery, the reader can sense a touch of parody in the narrator's announcement of Margarita's "real, true, eternal love." To write with full conviction about the redeeming power of love must have been a somewhat cynical act in post-revolutionary Russia. The narrator assumes the posture of a circus announcer before the reader, aware that the only way for redemption from the vulgar materialist condition and ideologized seriousness is through complete identification with the apparently illusory stereotypes of the romantic tradition. And most of the tricks work if the reader identifies with their fictional form and accepts that form as a fact which is beyond truth and falsity. Bulgakov is asking us openly to follow him, to trust him and the world of literary genres, which still possess a redeeming power for both writer and reader. Margarita is the source and focus of the space which evolves out of Bulgakov's demand for the absolute triumph of imagination over materialist logic. *The Master and Margarita* follows this fairy tale logic and works to transform the perception of the reader by leading him into the realm where literary convention, such as absolute love, defeats the positivist and scientific assumptions upon which the whole socialist realist tradition is founded.

Margarita's love for the Master is a projection of a craving for the utopian and paradisiacal state of being, which is usually derived from the idealization of the mother figure. Margarita is a vessel for this idea, and she is often portrayed as an idealized mother figure in relation to the Master and his art. The source of this love is the longing of the borderline writer for imaginary union with the maternal element, which denies the world of restrictions, prohibitions and borders imposed by the demands of a reality based on institutional organization. It is also worth noting that Margarita is childless and that the Master becomes a symbolic substitute for the child she desires and cannot have with her husband. The narrator's claim that, "of course she has not forgotten him," sounds more like a mother's concern than a lover's longing. Also, the physical relationship between the two of them is restricted to Margarita's stroking the Master's hair and worrying about his health, a relationship that reveals the pre-Oedipal tenderness of the mother who is still not completely separated from her child.

Margarita's love is a manifestation of a longing for a symbiotic union with the spiritual feminine element, which is supposed to redeem the Master from the suffering imposed by the restraints of the materialist ideology. On the other hand, the Master is a projection of a narcissistic personality who is not capable of love and reacts with disappointment and bitterness to every obstacle in external reality. In contrast to Margarita, the Master acts like the eternal adolescent who cannot find his place in the reality constructed by materialist ideology, but has a need to constantly invent his own, imaginary reality, which then becomes more real to him because he is aware of its illusory nature. This fictional reality is a refuge from the cruel realism of everyday life and therefore offers an escape for the writer. The mother-child relationship is the psychological basis for the success of their relationship since Margarita enjoys the imaginary space created by the Master's novel and the Master finds refuge in Margarita's rediscovery of that space, particularly when Woland helps them both in their ascent toward the transcendental plane where all the characters from the Master's novel exist eternally. The "upper scene" of the novel represents the imaginary space where all wish fulfillments are possible.

The fact that the novel, on both the "upper scene" and the "lower scene," evolves during the four nights of the full moon is not accidental. This is the time associated with ancient matriarchal fertility cults, which were later viewed by the Christians as diabolical rites. The demons help Margarita because she is ready to defy the dominant ideology and search for the Master, a condemned marginal writer. The powers of darkness, often identified with the feminine principle, serve those who have fallen out of favor with the dominant power structure. They all gather during Satan's ball, where Margarita plays the key role of queen or high priestess. This is a gathering of souls who have failed to obey the law of the higher, invisible god and are now subject to the domination of Woland. Margarita takes a blood bath and drinks Baron Meighel's blood from a human skull, invoking the pre-Christian ritual practices which are now contextualized as a rebellion of the feminine element against the dominant order. The demons aid Margarita in her quest for the Master because she abandons the law, turns into a witch, and pursues her desire to find her destitute lover. When she finally manages to restore the idyll of their early relationship and to return with him to his basement apartment, Margarita exclaims: "I'm so happy, so happy, happy that I made that bargain with him! Hurrah for the devil! I'm afraid, my dear, that you are doomed to live with a witch!" (*MM*, 353).

Margarita reveals the feminine element of Slavic culture, which resurges after the revolution and is empowered by the abolition of the patriarchal institution of the church. This element, which was part of Chernobog's domain in ancient Slavic culture, is first exploited and then suppressed by the Soviet ideologists after the revolution. In this imaginative novel, Bulgakov captures the shift from the values associated with the patriarchal reality principle to the anarchistic pleasure principle sublimated in Margarita's tender love. Her wild strength is born out of the defiance of rationalism and materialism that are officially enforced by the Soviet ideologists of the time. She is the source of the perpetual anarchic spirit which never settles for the here and now, but always yearns for the eternal and the transcendental value of human existence.

The betrayal of this idealist revolutionary spirit was evident in the Soviet Union by the 1930s, when the firm rule of a new Communist aristocracy was established under the sign of scientific socialism. The anarchistic spirit of the literary avant-garde, which was inspired by the same source, was replaced by the doctrine of socialist realism, which directly reflects the nature of the Stalinist doctrines in the fine arts. Margarita's love contradicts this restricted vision of reality and nourishes itself on the alliance with the dark powers, powers which allow her to help the Master and ascend into the world of the imagination that he has created for both of them. Margarita's magic flight has a tremendous impact on the whole novel: this is the moment when the material body is vanquished by the awakening demonic spirit of unrestrained freedom. Before her transformation, she is the modern cosmopolitan woman, who has everything in the material domain but continues actively to seek the experience which will awaken her other, spiritual nature. In her earthly aspect, she is a strong woman who is ready to defend herself against intruders, a fact that Azazello learns during their first encounter, while she is still not aware that he is not a pimp but a messenger from another world.

> "Swine!" she flung back at him over her shoulder. Immediately she heard the stranger's voice behind her:
> 'The mist that came from the Mediterranean Sea blotted out the city that Pilate so detested. . . . Jerusalem, the great city, vanished as though it had never been . . .' So much for your charred manuscript and your dried rose petals!" (*MM*, 221–22)

The only way for Azazello to come to terms with Margarita's wild temper is to quote straight from the Master's novel and show her that he is able to read her thoughts. Unlike Berlioz, who tries rationally to deny the existence of the other, invisible world, Margarita is persuaded as soon as she hears the words which are scribbled in the Master's handwriting on the remains of the part of the manuscript she has been able to save from the fire. This is the moment when she changes from the defensive, urban woman into a spirit guided by love. When she hears that her encounter with Woland may be instrumental in getting the information about the Master, she is ready to do anything. "I'll go!" Margarita burst out and seized Azazello by the arm. "I'll go wherever you like!" (*MM*, 223). Although Azazello does not tell her why the distinguished foreigner wants to meet her, Margarita is now ready to surrender completely for the sake of the Master. The overcoming of the rational egoist attitude is what ultimately earns a reward from the other world, both for her and the Master. Bulgakov's inversion of the stereotypical gender roles of the active male and the passive female creates the emotional basis for the transformation of the heroes. Margarita enters the "upper scene" of the novel by discarding her mundane self and by actively seeking the object of her desire. She then observes the demons and the Master as they are transformed on the "upper scene." "Margarita could not see herself, but she could see the change that had come over the Master. His hair had whitened in the moonlight and had gathered behind him into a mane that flew in the wind. Whenever the wind blew the Master's cloak away from his legs, Margarita could see the spurs that winked at the heels of his jackboots. Like the page demon the Master rode staring at the moon, though smiling at it as though it were a dear familiar friend . . ." (*MM*, 368–69).

Woland, Faggot, Behemoth, and Azazello change their carnivalesque outfits and appear in their medieval costumes. The Master is transformed from a mental patient wearing hospital pajamas into a medieval knight who joins the four Horsemen of the Apocalypse, led by Woland. Margarita, in the form now of divine wisdom, leads the Master out of his earthly misery into the realm of light that he had already imagined in his novel about Christ and Pilate. The reality of the "upper scene" and the imagination of the Master converge in the last chapter of the novel, which represents an apotheosis of the transcendental, immaterial principle of existence.

The stages of Margarita's heroic journey are projections of Bulgakov's "Slavic soul," the encoded mythological types of idealized femininity. The fact that "Margarita could not see herself" makes her into a complete ethereal presence on the higher plane of existence. She is disembodied, like a Byzantine Sophia, resurrected from her fallen, earthly state. Her final emanation is present in the last chapter only as a point of view, the central intelligence which witnesses the events of the Apocalyptic climax of the novel. Her compassion is so strong that she now tries to save Pontius Pilate, who is doing his "twenty-four thousand moons" penance for "one moon long ago," when he acted like a coward and allowed Kaiaphas to make a decision about Christ's execution (*MM*, 370). Margarita's moral transformation is characterized by the switch from retributive justice, which she applies to Latunsky while she is still immersed in the affairs on the "lower scene," to the higher justice based on forgiveness and compassion. The experience at Satan's ball transforms Bulgakov's heroine from a wild and aggressive force into an evolved form of idealized femininity. Margarita shows her compassion only after she has seen the sufferings of all the sinners that parade beside her at the ball. And even when Azazello offers to kill Latunsky, at the very end of her adventure with Woland, Margarita exclaims that such a thing is no longer necessary. She overcomes the standard moral judgement of right and wrong and identifies with all who are suffering, including the worst of criminals. She crosses the border which separates the two scenes and enters the higher realm, where the ethical principles of the "lower scene" no longer have any validity and everyone is forgiven in accordance with Christian ethics.

Margarita first passes from the state of boredom with her mundane existence to confrontation with her own aggressive and vengeful self once she has been given supernatural powers. But after the confrontation with the procession of damned souls at Satan's ball, she abandons the principle of power and extends her love for the Master to the whole suffering world. She gains a mystical insight into the story of Christ's suffering and understands the meaning of his message. Once she reaches the "upper scene," she begins closely to resemble the Christian image of the Mother of God. All traces of her demonic self now vanish. At the very end of the novel, after she bestows upon the Master his reward of eternal peace and silence, Margarita helps her beloved to overcome his "accursed memory." "Thus spoke Margarita as she walked with the Master toward their everlasting home, and Margarita's words seemed to him to flow like the whispering stream behind them, and the Master's memory, his accursed, needling memory, began to fade. He had been freed, just as he had set free the character he had created" (*MM*, 372).

The desire for the absolute, inherent in Bulgakov's ideological stance, emerges here as the utopian space which erases the memory of suffering in the material world. The Master regresses back to the paradisiacal state before the fall into the evil realm of the material world. He is freed from his memory just as "the character he had created" is freed from his own memory of the injustice he had done to Jesus Christ. Bulgakov is completely aware of the fictionality of such a proposition, but he nonetheless celebrates it as the only way for preserving the narcissistic space for the development of his art. "I shall watch over your sleep" (*MM*, 372) Margarita promises in the manner of an idealized maternal figure. At the end of the novel, she comes to represent the emptiness which subsumes, an entity without memory and therefore without guilt and morality. Her provision of the reward amounts to a return to the nonconflictual stage of absolute unity with the maternal. The whole novel, and most of the borderline tradition of the Slavic novel, develops in relationship to this feminine element in cultural practice. It is interesting that the feminine is incorporated as a positive element only in Bulgakov, who comes from a dominant, Russian culture. In other works analyzed in this study, the feminine, and especially the maternal, are coded as extremely negative forces which threaten the development of autonomous identity.

Bulgakov implies that the recovery of past memories can bring only a painful indication of the Master's insignificance and failure as a human being, while the eternal present, posited on the transcendental plane of the novel, provides the optimal space for the realization of his aesthetic ideals. This ahistorical attitude is motivated by the desire for the nonconflictual union with the maternal, where the distinction between subject and object is erased and every action takes place under the total control of the feminine element. This coding of the feminine in Slavic culture is a product of the dominant patriarchal attitude and has little to do with real women of that time. This identification with the maternal is the point at which similarities between the Eastern Orthodox Christianity, Communist ideology, and Bulgakov's borderline poetics start emerging. The kingdom of heaven, the classless society, and the total work of art all belong to the same category of ideological constructs which are motivated by the desire to merge with the maternal element in order to overcome the painful awareness of the passage of historical time and human finiteness. The Apocalyptic ending of the novel, which celebrates the imaginary salvation of the lovers on the "upper scene" and the destruction of the material world by fire, recalls the mythological elements which have influenced the shaping of Russian revolutionary ideology. The origins of the desire for the transcendental realm can be found in the gnostic rejection of the material world, which is equivalent to the psychological fantasy of return to the maternal space, preceding our existence in the world of history and language.

The emergence of the appropriated feminine element after the revolution finds its marginal, literary incarnation in Margarita's character. After the Christian religion of God the Father was officially abolished in the October Revolution, the ancient image of Damp Mother Earth was recycled. The revolutionary process awakened these dormant cultural forces, which originated in the images of Chernobog and were sublimated within the Mother of God in Orthodox Christianity. The new socialist institutions had no equivalent substitute for God the Father, able effectively to sublimate the huge excess of energy awakened by the revolution. Stalin's ideological role as Father of the People and an ideal mate for the feminized identity of the Soviet Union reversed the principles of unconditional love, upon which Eastern Christian ethics was founded. In reality, he acted as the incarnation of demonic forces, killing more then sixty million people while projecting an angelic image through *agitprop* ideology. His intention was to halt the revolutionary process and steer it in the direction of consolidation of his own power. In the process, he perverted and suppressed the potential the revolution had for the emancipation and liberation of both the material and spiritual creativity of the Russian people.

Margarita is the literary articulation of the other, suppressed aspect of the "Slavic soul," which was defeated after the establishment of Stalinism and replaced with the image of inert, passive, destructive femininity. Margarita's love is the projection of Bulgakov's hope that vulgar materialism can be overcome through amatory insight and spiritual transformation. Like the gnostic Sophia, Margarita acts as the Master's guide toward the absolute realm where love and forgiveness triumph and transform the bleak material world into a universe where the Master's literary fictions become validated.

The Master and Margarita is a novel that picks up the residues of the revolutionary process and shapes them into a literary vision which represents a powerful alternative to the collective dream of materialist ideology. It restructures the view of institutionalized Christianity into a parodic vision of human destiny, positing the literary imagination as a unique mode of being which allows for the exercise of anarchic freedom. It could be argued that Margarita's love creates a dimension that replaces the "opiate of the people" which has been abolished in the Soviet Union. Some form of "the opiate" proved to be more than necessary to manage the masses after the first revolutionary fervor subsided with the rise of Stalinism. In establishing rigid literary norms that prevented the writer from being a free poetic visionary and that required him to become an "engineer of the human soul," Stalinism failed to provide a successful substitute and produced only mediocre literature. The mechanistic view of man, espoused by the pioneers of Soviet science, viewed the human animal as the product of an interaction between physiology and history and failed to nurture the psychic space which was formerly occupied by the Christian concept of the soul. The existence of the individual was not regarded as valid outside the collective, ideological imagination which was dreamed up by Party ideologists. The Christian mythology was replaced by the Communist one, which stressed the importance of working on the material and technological improvement of the country. But the technological dream failed, and the work ethic never took root among the heirs of Marxism, who did not manage to invent the tool for the sublimation of creative energy as successfully as Christianity did.

The failure of materialist ideology to make the new socialist man who would be the unalienated subject of his own productivity was reflected in the field of literature. Literature in the service of ideology could probably please the ideologists, but it certainly did not manage to create the same impact that the novelists of the nineteenth century had outside the borders of Russia. After the unprecedented explosion of artistic innovation which characterized the first two decades of Russian cultural history in this century, the avant-garde practices were suffocated by the steel grip of Stalin's dictatorship. *The Master and Margarita* was the last gasp of the great imaginative tradition which successfully blended concerns of ideology, psychology, and literature and produced texts which became part of the world literary heritage. It is a dramatic example of the maxim that "man does not live by bread alone" and that the denial of his psychic and imaginative quality is equal to the destruction of his identity and personality.

mikhail bulgakov

Witold Gombrowicz:

Modernity, Gender, and Identity
in
Ferdydurke

While Mikhail Bulgakov derives his borderline poetics by regressing to the stereotypes of the romantic tradition, Witold Gombrowicz, a Polish novelist and playwright, rejects both the romantic heritage and the modern identity being forged from its remnants. Although both authors dismiss collective notions that occupy imagination and consciousness in this century and claim to embody the principle of the absolute freedom of personality, Gombrowicz pushes the border of artistic experiment a step further. He does not embrace the utopian dimension inherent in Bulgakov's parodic treatment of transcendental literary heaven, inscribed on the "upper scene" of *The Master and Margarita,* but continues to ridicule every aspiration to mastery and stable identity inherent in the logic of the literary canon and its creators. His disgust with the academic elite, which exercises its critical muscle by enforcing historical and theoretical versions of literature as an institution, is the existential foundation of Gombrowicz's borderline poetics. In the 1954 entry of his diary, Gombrowicz claims that it was irritation with the "thousand idiotic assessments" of the literary inquisitors that provoked him to write *Ferdydurke*.

> Today, years later, when I am a lot calmer, less at the mercy and the lack of mercy of judgements, I think about the basic assumptions of *Ferdydurke* regarding criticism and I can endorse them without reservation. There are enough innocent works that enter life looking as if they did not know that they would be raped by a thousand of idiotic assessments! . . . Yet defense against these opinions is possible only when we manage a little humility and admit how important they really are to us, even if they come from an idiot. . . . This fiction is absurd and the truth, the difficult and tragic truth is that the idiot's opinion is also significant. It also creates us, shapes us from inside out, and has far reaching practical and vital consequences.[1]

Ferdydurke is a novel written in response to these "assessments" of the literary critics who assume the position of social and moral superiority as members of an academically or socially prestigious institution. But, unlike Bulgakov's Master who completely depends on the maternal dimension of Margarita's character to achieve the transcendence of the vulgar materialist universe, Gombrowicz dispenses entirely with the romantic identity of the Faustian artist and attempts to embrace and transcend all the contradictions inherent in the modern civilization through an autobiographical literary performance. Existential situations are the perpetual parodic podium for the display of the pain and suffering imposed on him by the literary inquisitors who destroy his "innocent works."

In the first chapter of *Ferdydurke,* entitled "Abduction," the narrator explains how he had been naive enough to try to enter the world of serious and mature adults by writing a book called *Memoirs of a Time of Immaturity.* But instead of the desired stability and acceptance by the literary establishment, a torrent of opinions overwhelms him. "It is like being born in a thousand rather narrow minds" (*F,* 17).[2] Instead of honoring his sincere desire to address the problem of immaturity and the "lower part of our person," a counterpart of our serious and adult selves, literary inquisitors, disguised as "cultural aunts," reprimand him for writing such an extreme and problematic book. The narrator, for his part, instead of promising how to correct his faults and heartily embrace maturity, decides to hurl himself even deeper into infantilism and undermine every attempt at serious and lofty assessment of his work. *Ferdydurke* is the final product of this endeavor—an ode to the eternal power of immaturity to distort and undermine "civilized identity," an abstraction that he believes is founded on mutual agreement and worship of conventions.

The novel was first published in Warsaw in 1937, causing a literary sensation and scandal two years before the Nazi invasion of Poland. Gombrowicz emigrated to Buenos Aires just before the invasion and lived in relatively anonymous exile for the next twenty-four years. Twenty years after the original publication of *Ferdydurke,* Polish authorities allowed it to be republished in Warsaw. In 1957, ten thousand copies were sold in a few days in Warsaw. But the thaw didn't last long. Many of the ideas touched upon by Gombrowicz in *Ferdydurke* had been actualized in the totalitarian dictatorships that dominated East-Central Europe, after the invasion of Nazi and Communist ideologies. "Cultural aunts" were now wearing commissars' boots in Poland—the Party decided that Gombrowicz's parody could easily be applied to any institutional structure, including the Communist one. In 1958, Gombrowicz's name was erased from Polish registers. But the Parisian literary scene had already picked up the signals about the work of the Slavic novelist, whose poetics had anticipated many of the ideas developed by the French existentialists in the 1950s.

Ferdydurke is based on a parody of the entire Western metaphysical tradition, culminating in the technology of terror during the World Wars. The apparent frivolity of chapter five, "Philifor Honeycombed with Childishness," the narrative function of which defies the rules of the novelistic genre, reveals the flimsy foundations of the Western intellectual tradition. The episode involves a duel between Dr. Philifor, "the higher synthethist," and Anti-Philifor, "the professor of higher analysis," both aspiring dictators in their respective scientific viewpoints. The analyst reduces the synthethist's wife into a chaos of parts; in turn, the synthethist offers progressively larger sums of money in order to structure the moral setup of licentious Fiora Gente, the analyst's female companion. The contestants end up

witold gombrowicz

decomposing and recomposing their significant others, trying to demonstrate their own intellectual power and metaphysical validity. The battle is always externalized, waged on the other side of the boundary of the self. While the women are being constructed and deconstructed through the powers of synthesis and analysis, the two professors remain narcissistically enclosed in their own world of ideas, personalities, and ultimately their involvement with each other. After their women expire from the experiments, the two contestants end up together, their spiritual romance culminating in the "firing at what they could with what they could" (*F,* 100).

Gombrowicz goes to very root of the structuralist contradiction, showing the shameless Manicheism that confronts the monologic force engendered by Christianity. The absurdity and falsity of binary thought is displayed as an exaggerated, inhuman fixation that haunts living human beings. The professors appear as laughable puppets from the popular theater, moved by the invisible hand of the opposed ideologies of "analysis" and "synthesis." They are dragged down from their positions of eminence because of their pathetic desire for absolute knowledge, which turns them into infantile dictators and destructive fools in the Gombrowiczian literary universe. That universe is a violent, nightmarish procession of ideological mirages, explosively produced by the author's clash with the dominant codes. "And reality, battered and exhausted too, became a world of dreams—oh! escape into dream" (*F,* 48). Dreams fashion reality because the latter is weakened by the onslaught of political propaganda. This is a foundation of Gombrowicz's borderline poetics: "To persons interested in my writing technique, I offer the following recipe: Enter the realm of dreams."[3] This fascination with the unconscious operations of ideology leads to a failure of all stable identities. Each character is striving toward the ideal embodiment of the one and only socially acceptable role. But, as soon as that role is seriously engaged, the infantile tendency that refuses to identify with ideals erupts and causes parodic laughter.

The achievement of mature, normal identity is perceived by Gombrowicz as a surrender of individual authenticity, a moral price that he is not willing to pay. The structure of *Ferdydurke* is founded

on the desire to cross the border of the ideologically constructed
identity and affirm an anarchic individuality without boundaries.
Gombrowicz is aware that such a radical break with the accepted
norms of reality is doomed to failure since the formation of a new
ideological mask is inevitable. The characters in the novel provoke
laughter in the cynical reader because they tend to display their ideology in order to overcome "immaturity." Behind every ideological
mask, Gombrowicz sees a face with pimples that refuses to be molded
according to a mature, adult identity.

unmasking ideology

Thirty-year-old Johnny Kowalsky, the main protagonist of *Ferdydurke,*
narrates his search for a sincere human face in three different mono-
logues. The first is a nightmarish regression to boyhood and school.
In the second, Johnny tells about his attempts to destabilize the family of Moderns, his adopted family, which is supposed to re-educate
him in accordance with the latest trends in cosmopolitan living and
humanist ideology. The final sequence takes place in the Polish countryside, where Johnny searches for a stable-lad, the country boy with
a simple human face. All he finds are retarded gentry and peasants
who turn into dogs. The novel ends with a parody of a romantic
denouement: Johnny falls in love with a girl cousin who resembles a
type of female found in dentists' waiting rooms. Between Johnny's
adventures, which comprise the novel's main storyline, Gombrowicz
inserts critical meditations and comical sketches about Philifor and
Philimor. Three acts of the main drama, with an intermezzo and the
critical introduction to this intermezzo, simulate the structural order
of a theatrical performance. The characters are never "real people"
living in a "real world," but actors on the stage set by Gombrowicz's
vision of humanity. The characters are explicitly shaped like the ideological masks that humans are forced to wear by the mysterious force
that Gombrowicz calls the "interhuman space." This space of interhuman communication is the moment when the involved parties
reach the point where they have to decide to start agreeing or

disagreeing about certain ideological postures. They have to leave the space of primary narcissism in order to embrace something grandiose and abstract. The secondary narcissism of ideology forces them to become something that they are not. "We shall soon begin to be afraid of ourselves and our personalities, because we shall discover that they do not completely belong to us" (*F,* 284). The moment one personality enters into dialogue with another, the theatrical forces are unleashed and they both act out the ideological material with which they have been indoctrinated.

The stage of *Ferdydurke* is dominated by ideologies propelling nations in the direction of war. For Gombrowicz these ideologies represent the "demoniacal forces of formal mobilization. The Nazis and the Communists fashioned menacing, fanatical masks for themselves; the fabrication of faiths, enthusiasms, and ideals resembled the fabrication of cannons and bombs" (*F,* 282). The ideology of power, in both its right- and left-wing formulations, leads humanity to massive self-destruction. At the same time, power ideology plays a crucial role in politically subduing the autonomy of intellectual expression. "Blind obedience and blind faith had become essential and not only in the barracks" (*F,* 282). Everyone is obliged to participate in the theater of cruelty, acting out the monstrous roles assigned by the new, emerging faiths. Gombrowicz assumes the role of the cynical prophet: "I discovered man's reality in this unreality to which he is condemned" (*F,* 283). For Gombrowicz, "unreality" represents the paralysis of thought by the irrational demands of ideology and maturity, a moment when dream logic conquers reason and begins to fashion new models for identification. "Reality begins where the state and its terminology end."[4]

Ferdydurke is a monument to the unreality and irrationality of ideologically constructed civilization. The initial narrative sequence ends with a duel of grimaces in the classroom of a Polish grammar school. Siphon, the embodiment of teachers' ideals, the student who cherishes his own innocence and boyishness, is confronted by Mientus, a rebellious adolescent in search of a face without a grimace. Siphon is the perfect material for a model citizen; Mientus is a proto-anarchist. Schoolboys organize a contest with firm rules: "The two contestants will stand facing each other and will make a series of faces. Each and every constructive and beautiful face made by Siphon will be answered by an ugly and destructive counter-face by Mientus. The faces made will be as personal and as wounding as possible, and the contestants will continue to make them until a final decision is reached" (*F,* 65).

As soon as the signal is given for the contest to begin, the narrator has an attack of unreality: "At these words the reality burst from its frame, unreality turned into nightmare, the whole improbable adventure became a dream in which I was imprisoned with no possibility of even struggling" (*F,* 65). The narrator walks the border between dream and reality, tormented by the power of form that coerces him to act out ideas much larger then his own personality. He feels trapped in a situation in which he is forced to witness the educational methods of the demonic Inspector Pimko and other guardians of cultural values. As Pimko reads the initial paragraphs of Johnny's book, Johnny feels the imposing presence of the literary inquisitor. "Something terrible was happening inside and yet outside me, something absurd, something impudently unreal" (*F,* 23). The narrator's perspective is constantly disrupted by shocks that take place in a space without a definite border, "inside and yet outside me." The border between the individual identity and ideologically constructed reality has been erased or made invisible by the "cultural aunts" who enforce the dominant ideology in the subtlest possible way.

Guided by good intentions, the inspector orders the thirty-year-old Johnny to go back to the second grade and relearn how to "decline mensa, mensam, mensae and conjugate amo, amas, amat" (*F,* 24). Latin is the language of intellectual oppression, the idiom of high culture, introduced into Polish history by the Catholic church. Boys are forced to sublimate their sexual curiosity by repeating conjugations and declinations. Pimko is at the same time provoking them to use bad language and obscene words. This only increases their guilt. Posing as a priest, the schoolmaster tempts them into sin, so that he could later claim their youthful souls. Boys are portrayed as spoiled simpletons whose education is founded on mental torture by the state and church. This alienating force is opposed by the pseudoromantic notion of pagan Slavic stable-lads, who presumably live in complete accord with the natural environment. The sublimation

witold gombrowicz

of the body and its shameful functions, through the adoration of a falsified image of "natural man," invokes basic mistrust in Gombrowicz. The literary mystification of the body crumbles when Johnny and Mientus, the ego and the id of the text, discover that the stable-lad is actually closer to the dog than to a human being. "Mientus walked round the clamp one way and I walked another (to the accompaniment of deafening, frantic barking from the neighboring hovels), and we found the peasant, as well as his wife and the quadruplets she was feeding from one anaemic dog (the other had long since become unserviceable). They barked desperately and furiously and tried to run away, but Mientus chased the peasant and caught him" (*F,* 203).

The romantic mask of rustic Slavic peasant crumbles when Mientus and Johnny encounter his threatening animality. Mientus "catches him" like a noble hunter trying to capture the wild beast whose image awakens strange curiosity in his mind. The ideological division between the nobleman and the peasant erupts in the last episode of the novel. Peasants are ruthlessly vital, truly beyond good and evil, since they never fully assimilate the Catholic ideology. To be a noble is to act like a retarded child, who has to be dressed, fed, and taken places by the peasant servants. Gombrowicz manages to represent in a parodic, theatrical manner the clash between these two types of class consciousness. The Hegelian-Marxist master-slave dialectic is represented here in a tone of extreme cynicism, as a struggle of existential masks that cannot be resolved by identification. His parody is a cathartic critique of ideology from a cynical distance, a posture that allows him to imagine a recuperation from the engulfment by the totality of social norms. The class struggle is transformed into a carnival, its seriousness is mocked, and its protagonists are reduced to cartoonish images.

The two class masks—the city boy without a stable identity and the stable-lad who embodies plump, rosy-cheeked simplicity—clash and stare at each other without a trace of understanding. This is enough to worry old Uncle Edward, the landed gentlemen who is wilting in the desolation of the Polish countryside. He suspects that Mientus is "the victim of childish mania influenced by Bolshevik propaganda" (*F,* 246). Mientus' desire to "fra . . . ternize" with the stable-lads, to finally reach beyond the mask and find the true, sincere human face, is read by Uncle Edward as showing the influence of Communist propaganda. Uncle Edward finds that the Communist goal of a classless society is really rooted in adolescent idealism, in Mientus's "childish mania." The desire of the disenfranchised city boy to identify with a low class person, to throw away the burden of academic knowledge and enjoy the "freedom" of the peasant lad, stems from his inability to identify with any of the models that are offered to him by urban living. "Communism. Fascism. Catholic Youth Movement. Patriotic Youth Movement. Youth Morality Movement. Boy Scouts. Civic Youth Movement. Heroic Youth Movement. More and more far-fetched words and phrases were launched into fray. It was obvious that each political party stuffed these boys' heads with a different idea of boyhood, that every thinker stuffed them with his own particular tastes and ideals, and that over and above all that their heads were stuffed with films, popular novels, and newspapers" (*F,* 51).

The image of the boy's head, stuffed with popularized versions of ideologies that were to invade Poland in the next several years, terrifies with its acute, exaggerated quality. Youth is immersing itself in the world of politics, culture, and information in order to escape the terrifying idea of lonely individuality. The boys are joining various ideological camps to rid themselves of youthful awkwardness and immaturity. In the process, they trade their own personalities for a larger, ideological vision of their place in the system of social and political hierarchies and turn into monstrous caricatures of adulthood and maturity. The repertoire of identities contained in the heritage of the whole of Western Civilization is not sufficient to satisfy a single pimply adolescent. Gombrowicz treats ideological constructs of culture as the alienating force that inserts itself between man and the world. The images of adjustment and success that are projected conjunctively with swastika or with hammer and sickle provoke horror in the author, who can foresee the catastrophic outcome of this shameless manipulation of youth.

In order to draw closer to an authenticity he cannot imagine, Johnny is forced to seek his identity in models opposed to the dominant ideological images of adjusted youth: uneducated peasants or

witold gombrowicz

rebellious dropouts. Everyone who belongs to the zone of subculture is a model worth exploring. This is the first step in the protagonist's descent to the depths of immaturity and absurdity. He does not want to be "stuffed" with the ideals, he wants to always embrace the distance and void of the recluse. He defends his miserable individuality and allows himself to sink low in order to show his autonomy and independence. Johnny assumes the ultimate existential posture of withdrawal from everyday life into the narcissistic comfort of writing. It is as if Gombrowicz were trying to prove that it is better to be associated with the low elements of society and have a personality of one's own than to participate in the hypocritical social masquerade of the higher classes. This descent into the region of subculture, into a world independent of the high cultural values of aristocracy and bourgeoisie, represents the definitive break with literary canons and institutions. Gombrowicz rejects the social norms of the higher classes, derived from the amalgam of Catholic hypocrisy and nationalist megalomania, and embraces the underworld, engendered from the darker, less formalized mythological material of pre-Christian times preserved among the lower classes. He demonstrates how the serious, mature cultural values turn into their opposite when they are elevated into the zone of the immortal, monolithic high culture. The chapter entitled "Introduction to Philifor Honeycombed with Childishness," which is one of the interludes inserted into the main narrative of Johnny's existential trials, is entirely devoted to the narrator's critical meditations on the narcissistic delusions of the "world's artistic circles." "But the things that happen in the world's artistic circles beat all records in stupidity and ignominy—to such an extent that it is impossible for a normally constituted and balanced person not to sweat with shame in the presence of their childish and pretentious orgies" (*F,* 75).

The existential mask of the artist, or the second-rate artist, as Gombrowicz likes to define him, is formed by the desire to identify with the immortals who constitute the artistic canon of our civilization. But instead of trying to discover the unique quality of their existential situation, these eternal aspirants to greatness end up being "quarter Chopins and half Shakespeares" (*F,* 76). What offends the narrator of *Ferdydurke* even more is that these incarnations of mediocrity then form literary clubs where they engage in "mutual congratulations, organizing dinners, always seeking new lies to justify the suspect reason for their existence" (*F,* 76). This situation is the breeding ground of hypocrisy, since congratulations are false and the participants end up despising one another and themselves in particular, whereas the writer ought to be expressing an existential reality by exposing the various obligatory postures in the masquerade produced by social, political, and literary institutions. "For he who is placed in a false and artificial situation cannot utter a single word that is not false and artificial, and whatever he says, does, or thinks necessarily turns against him and does him harm" (*F,* 78).

The falsity of this situation breeds a literature that hardly touches upon anything considered by Gombrowicz as the significant element of one's existential situation. The significant elements are the degradation and immaturity experienced when faced with the models society offers as ideals for identification. Gombrowicz's borderline poetics necessarily takes the form of disclosing the artificiality of the human situation in the reality constructed by the overt propaganda of various political interests. The unmasking is purposely frivolous, since humor enables the author to overcome the pain of existence without a stable identity. "Frivolity is not to be avoided; for we learnt long ago to use humor to evade matters that we find too painful" (*F,* 73). The inability to confront the pain and the desire to escape from it are the psychological mechanisms that motivate *Ferdydurke.* The fear of pain does not allow the author to struggle against the overt ideologization of reality, but forces him to keep an ironic distance and "take refuge in misplaced laughter" (*F,* 73). He firmly believes that the struggle has already been lost, that the absolute has been dissolved into a chaotic jumble of unrelated pieces, and that the ideological masks the youths are forced to wear instead of faces are just a futile attempt at restoring this absolute. "But let us also note that the laws and principles of construction to which we are subject are themselves only the production of the part, and an insignificant part into the bargain—a tiny segment of the world, a microcosm scarcely bigger than one's little finger, a minute group of specialists and aesthetes all of whom could be crowded into a teaspoon, whose relentless pressure on each other results in the distillation of ideas of even greater subtlety" (*F,* 73).

Art is no longer able to grasp the totality of the life process, since the unshakeable center of the medieval universe has been displaced by the modern ideologies of change, progress, and nationalism. Technology replaces spirituality, and art, the last refuge of the spiritual, is doomed to marginalization, appreciated only by the corrupted elite of aesthetes. The philosophical dismantling of metaphysics in the past century, mainly by the fathers of modern thought, Marx and Nietzsche, has resulted in the material destruction of humanist civilization in two World Wars. The totality of God's world has been finally shattered and only its parts can now be grasped by the specialist, who distills them into "ideas of even greater subtlety."

The psychological and political problem of fragmentation of both individual consciousness and social reality is the source of Gombrowicz's torments. His internal (and eternal) adolescent demands that the totality of both psyche and society be kept intact. This absolutist demand of youth is not sated by the hypocrisy of the mask, since it hungers for the truth of experience in a fashion similar to that of Diogenes.[5]

youth and modernity

The fear of aging, dying, and fossilization is another unconscious determinant of Gombrowicz's borderline posture. In order to preserve the internal adolescent, he undertakes the painful task of self-objectivization in language. He admires both the concept and the embodiment of youth as the source of his own cultural anarchism. "I have to confess this: under the influence of the war, the strengthening of the 'inferior' and regressive powers, an eruption of some sort of belated youth took place in me. I fled to youth in the face of defeat and slammed the door. I had always had the inclination to seek in youth, that is, in my youth and that of others, a haven from 'values,' that is, from culture. I have already written in this diary: youth is a value in itself, that is, a destroyer of all other values, which are not necessary to it because it is self-sufficient."[6]

This confession of an exile, thousands of miles from Poland where his brother had already been sent to a concentration camp, amounts to a psychopathological diagnosis of the Second World War. The glorification of youth by the Nazis affects the whole of Europe and causes regression to a stage where aggressive action against the world of "old culture" and "values" becomes laudable. If there is a value that Gombrowicz sides with, it is the youth, his own and that of others. Youth, as he says, is a value that is autonomous precisely because it is "a destroyer of all other values." It is not difficult to recognize the traumatic effects of war, which was supposed to carry out the National-Socialist pledge of "rejuvenating" Western Civilization through the sacrifice of the old world of an "international Jewish conspiracy," to be performed by the blond, northern European youth. This historical regression, caused by the inability of an exhausted intellectual tradition to find a proper cultural and political placebo after the weakening of religious and humanist sublimatory mechanisms, erupts in the "higher race" orgy, which glorified youth, simplicity, and work. The melancholy, decadence, and spirit of resignation, which characterized the interwar period in Europe, were wiped out by the Nazi occupiers as part of the old, corrupt world. The parody of all cultural forms arises from the same disenchantment with European cultural senility and a hankering after youth, which Gombrowicz, like the Nazis, discovers in the repressed homosexual admiration of boyish innocence. "Youth. I could say that I was looking for both my own and somebody else's youth. Someone else's because the youth in a naval or soldier's uniform, the youth of those archcommon boys from the Retiro, was inaccessible, their sex, the lack of sexual attraction, excluded the possibility of joining and possessing. My own because it was also mine, it came to life in someone like me, not in a woman, but in a man, this was the same youth that had cast me off, now blossoming in someone else."[7]

Gombrowicz, like a parodic version of Thomas Mann's Aschenbach, rediscovers his own youth not in Venice, but in Buenos Aires, and understands that it is no longer accessible to him as a living, existential experience. The sense of loss of one's own youth is compensated through this vampiric, specular symbiosis with "the youth in a naval or soldier's uniform." The uniform, the fetish of identification, enables Gombrowicz to behold the youth as a "value in itself," devoid of all personal characteristics, which could only be obstacles in his project of forgetfulness. In order to stop the passage of time and affirm the omnipresence of youth, the homosexual imagination constantly recycles the world of male bodies without a personal form, bodies that possess one uniform characteristic— isomorphism and youth. The inability to identify with the cultural values of his time leads Gombrowicz into a narcissistic glorification of his own youthful self, which is then generalized to the world of boys, where it comes to life again and again.

The narcissism and homosexuality that underlie Nazi ideology, the denial of difference, whether sexual or racial, finds a peculiar articulation in Gombrowicz. His poetics is extremely individualistic, and similarities with a mass political movement are due to certain historical, cultural, and political contexts against which he places his writings. He gives expression to the psychopolitical turmoil of his age by acting out the ideological forces that transform European cultural identity into a monstrous eruption of violence. The laughter provoked by his parodies is demonic and bitter at the same time. By rejecting culture, history, and ideology, he becomes their victim: by consciously rejecting identification, he unconsciously reflects the darkest desires of his age. He is masochistic enough to desire to share the destiny of the degraded peasant boys, but at the same time sadistic enough to never let go of his own sense of literary mastery.

"And I, Ferdydurke, repeated the third section of my book, the story of Mientus who tries to fraternize with a stable boy."[8] Gombrowicz becomes his own biographer and confesses that the writing of *Ferdydurke* is an explicit autobiographical elaboration of his disguised homosexuality. He admires the youthful face that is not wrinkled by any social mask or gesture, the vulnerable and puerile face that conquers him because it is socially low and degraded. His fascination with the Buenos Aires youth is increased by their rural origin: "Here, youth, already degraded as youth, was subjected to a second degradation, as rural youth, proletarian youth."[9] Gombrowicz, who misrepresented himself as a Polish count to Buenos Aires society, suffers the destiny of the disenchanted elite. He falls in love with youth across the class boundary and worships the stable-lad whose destiny is still not formed by the iron codes of noble behavior. He would like to cross over and experience freedom, but realizes that by worshiping the stable-boy he is betraying his desire to be an aristocrat and to possess him totally.

The youth of the stable-lad comes alive "not in a woman, but in a man," because identification with a woman would mean departure from the narcissistic enclosure of one's own sex. The understanding of difference is not available to Gombrowicz, who practices an absolute rejection of ideology followed by megalomaniac enlargement of his own ego. He understands writing as an act of parodic self-mythologization, a way of remaining true only to his own desire and vision.

Miss Youthful, the golden child of the modern family where Johnny is sent for re-education, is the first female figure to demonstrate different models of youth. "She was young twice over—by reason of her age and by reason of her modernity; that was it, she was young because of her youth" (*F*, 105). Johnny's first reaction to the encounter with Miss Youthful is fear of losing control over his own destiny. Like a true borderline personality, the narrator fears anything that can break the imaginary web of his delusions and withdraws further and further into the madness of his own novel. "Consequently I was terrified by being confronted with something stronger than myself, and still more terrified when I saw that it was not she who was afraid of the professor, but the professor who was afraid of her" (*F*, 105). Her cool manners and modernity quickly dispel the learned arrogance of professor Pimko, leaving Johnny without parental guidance in his duel with a modern girl. Her youth is not authentic for Gombrowicz, because she is a woman and because she is the symbol of difference that terrifies him, being uncontrollable and unknown. Pimko, the repository of old patriarchal values, launches a campaign against the modern girl, fearing that he may lose Johnny's "little backside" (*pupa* in Polish) to her. The ideology of modernism, founded on Gombrowicz's adoration of youth, becomes the target of Pimko's demagogy. "And he launched into terrible flattery of my alleged youth and modernism, saying more or less that we young people were interested only in legs, and flattering us in other ways, while the girl went on picking her face with the most complete indifference, totally oblivious to what was going on behind her back" (*F,* 108).

It is "the most complete indifference" of Miss Youthful that irritates the narrator. She has assimilated the imperatives of "youth and modernity" so completely that nothing can move her from the self-sufficient attitude that contemporary culture permits. Unlike Johnny, who is forced into regression by Pimko, her identity is a hybrid of the new cult of youth. She is presented as an athletic body, without feelings, guilt, or morality. Unlike Mientus and Johnny, the leading male protagonists of the novel, she appears to be invulnerable in her cool indifference. While the boys agonize because they are unable to find any model for identification, Miss Youthful assimilates the modern cult of youth, as if she were sucking it in through a straw. Her mother, Mrs. Youthful, whom Gombrowicz characterizes in a derogatory manner as "the she-graduate," is the main support for her daughter's modernity. This new philosophy of education, enforced by the mothers, brings Johnny to additional torments. "Moreover, the enterprising female graduates of the present day, inflamed by collectivism and emancipation, detest artificiality and pretence in the young, and above all cannot stand their posing for grown-ups. As progressives with their faces turned towards the future, they make a greater cult of youth than it has ever previously enjoyed; and nothing irritates them more than seeing a young person sullying his youth by adopting poses" (*F,* 111).

This vision of youth arising out of popularized versions of modern living, unconsciously enforced by the subtlest operations of ideology, transforms Miss Youthful into the aesthetic ideal of a perfect body without the unnecessary burden of a doubting mind. She is a product of the new generation that does not question its existential authenticity, but accepts what is given and rejects thought. The dogma of progress and orientation toward the future is a feature not only of the extreme versions of communism and Nazism, but also a foundation of European bourgeois culture. Mrs. Youthful uses the "modernism-anachronism" formula to place Johnny in the category of poseurs, those young people who sully their youth by rejecting a straightforward, honest, sincere relationship to the world around them (*F,* 112). Of course, nobody realizes that Johnny is actually thirty years old and that he has a clear perception of Miss Youthful's straightforwardness as just another mask.

The ideology of modernism is transformed into this ultimate mask, which the whole Youthful family wears in the novel. Their liberal manners are imported from the other side of the border, from the centers for the dissemination of modern culture. Johnny exhibits the complexes of a secondary culture when he fails to fascinate and seduce Miss Youthful. "She would certainly prefer having an American boy-friend in the house to a miserable, old-fashioned, grudge-bearing poseur" (*F,* 122). Polish identity is hidden behind the mask of modern pragmatism, imported to Europe along with American products. Miss Youthful's "natural pose" reminds Johnny of the advertising image of "American girls sitting on the sides of their motor-boats" (*F,* 122). The behavior of the "modern" schoolgirl is so magical and magnetic that Johnny's adult identity is immediately under siege. "To be swallowed whole by a modern schoolgirl, and never to be able to find a single fault with her style or detect the slightest chink or cranny which held out the prospect or possibility of flight, liberation, escape" (*F,* 134). The engulfment by the feminine is feared since it means the loss of youth and autonomy. Falling in love with modernity, which finds its dominant expression in the athletic body of the Polish girl, is a terrifying experience for Johnny Kowalsky. It is this act of identification with the beloved that he fears, an identification that comes too easily for one who still has doubts about his own identity. "I too grew red in the face and shouted: 'Modernism forever! Up with the modern boy! Up with the modern girl!'" This parodic performance of the narrator discloses the origins of Gombrowicz's poetic practice. The subject of the text tries to hold on to the infantile experience of the narcissistic, self-reflecting void,

witold gombrowicz

enclosed within the expansive boundless individuality. But the boundaries of style and culture come after the subject, disguised as the seducing demonic forms that "devour" his borderline identity. The narrator gives up that provisional, infantile identity quite easily, since he cannot understand the nature of psychological defenses. He acts out the dominant ideology of his age in spite of himself and speaks out from a position of apathetic withdrawal because "it becomes impossible for anyone to distinguish between the real and the unreal, between truth and fiction, between the felt and the unfelt, between the natural and the artificial, the pretentious and the false" (*F,* 129). The blurring of boundaries creates a space into which the dream logic with its demands for the absolute rule of imagination can infiltrate. Gombrowicz openly desires to subdue both characters and implicitly his readers to the dictums of his own imagination.[10] This desire becomes manifest in the narrator's war cries against the modernity of the Youthful family. At one point in the novel, Johnny hires a beggar to stand on the street in front of the Youthfuls' home with a green twig in his mouth. When Mrs. Youthful is perplexed by this performance, Johnny openly expresses his belligerence. "At her! After her! Pursue! Strike! Capture! Slave of my imagination, victim of my whim" (*F,* 148). When the girl's modern indifference is shaken by the absurd scene in front of her window, the narrator becomes wildly excited. She is finally reacting to his presence, noticing a senseless act of an old man standing in front of her with a branch protruding from his mouth. His aggression is comical, but it is nevertheless an assault on the girl and on her values.

This travesty of a military assault disguises the aggression that guides Gombrowicz's literary practice. The poetic drive is motivated by the anarchism of the subject in constant suspension. Gombrowicz strives after absolute youth and irresponsibility, destroying one mask after another, until the disorder of infantile laughter dissolves them all. The beggar with a green twig in his mouth is a perfect symbol of the attempt to impose his own irrationality by manipulating those who are the victims of the modernist ideology. In trying to get rid of his love for the modern girl, Johnny is aware that "the green bitterness in the beggar's buccal cavity" is "in too great a conflict with a modern vision of the world" (*F*, 148). The aggression disguised by the parodic, distorted vision of reality reaches its culmination in the fantasies of the girl's destruction and dismemberment. "In the end I actually reached a state of dreaming of the girl's physical destruction, of disfiguring her pretty little face, injuring her, cutting off her nose" (*F*, 135). Immediately, the narrator refrains from the actual use of physical violence, since "the mind can free itself only by its own efforts" (*F*, 135). The external environment is never real enough for active participation in it; therefore, it is the power of imagination that Gombrowicz has to use in order to involve and seduce others by his own infantile vision of the world.

His rebellion against maturity demonstrates both the political and the psychological determinants of the "modern vision of the world." When Johnny is alone in the Youthful household, he explores the rooms and analyzes the symbols used by modern youth to express its vitality and independence. He is especially fascinated by the girl's bedroom, which betrays a modern insistence on the dynamic nature of life. "It reflected the contemporary hurry and bustle, the girl's nomadism, a kind of carpe diem feeling, connected by secret underground passages to the free-and-easy, hurrying nature of modern youth in the motor age" (*F*, 151). The superficiality, the lack of guilt and of spiritual depth produced by it, only enhance Miss Youthful's power and beauty. "That I, tormented by idealist youth, should thirst so greatly for this ideal should surprise nobody" (*F*, 134). His thirst is spiced with a touch of aggression, with an obsessive desire to denigrate and discredit the perfection of the modern family. He enters the bedroom of Mr. and Mrs. Youthful and feels offended by its hygienic flavor. "I stood there for a long time, sniffing the atmosphere, analyzing its constituent parts, trying to find the clue to the prevalent bad taste, to find a way of fouling the whole environment" (*F*, 149). Something in the narrator rebels against the apparent perfection of the modern family; a part of him is disgusted by the way Western fashions are shaping the destinies of his countrymen.

Besides modernity, Gombrowicz has a very difficult time reconciling himself to his Polishness. The Polish complex is the product of a splitting of the presymbolic, pagan identity in the medieval world of symbolic differences between nobility and peasants. The Catholic and Latin culture dominated the Polish nobility and made them into worshipers of things foreign. At the same time, the illiterate masses of Polish peasants continued to live in the worlds of Slavic folk culture and of Latin sacred culture. The secondary culture complex starts with the inability of the nobles to completely reproduce Roman Catholic institutional organizations. The immature, pagan element would always erupt as a "demon of verdure" that plagues the installation of the foreign, Catholic culture. The dominant Polish culture, never satisfied with its heathen authenticity, always tries to detach itself from its rustic, Slavic roots and prove to Europe and the world that it is more than an equal.[11] Johnny tries to defeat the refined modernity of the Youthfuls through a display of disgusting and socially inappropriate behavior. While at the dinner table, Johnny deliberately eschews good table manners. "So, to consolidate myself in my pitiful condition and to demonstrate the extent of my utter indifference to everything, my total unworthiness, I started putting bread crumbs, scraps of lettuce, and so on into my fruit salad, and stirring the mixture with my finger" (*F,* 141). Johnny's infantile performance exposes both his personal immaturity and the false pretenses of the elite part of Polish culture that denies its origins so blindly. The narrator of *Ferdydurke* assumes an entirely abject posture to undermine the Youthfuls, who believe that they are as progressive as the Western Europeans. In the process they manifest the Polish complex. But Gombrowicz insists on a different way of constructing and appreciating the fragile cultural identity of a Central European. "The Pole, formed by Poland, by the Polish environment and tradition, is necessarily a less sophisticated man than the Westerner" (*F,* 281). This admission of inferiority is not a defeat, but an acceptance of a historically constructed cultural identity.

Gombrowicz himself never fully resolved his Polish complex, which surfaced in Argentina. Describing his unsuccessful attempts to fit into the literary society of Buenos Aires, he asks a rhetorical question: "And wasn't I, after all, a Pole and didn't they know that Poles are not, generally, finos, and generally not on the level of Parisian issues."[12] The interesting thing about the Polish complex is that it is not only a psychological phenomenon and that it is not only characteristic of Poland. In fact, the historical and political conditions of the entire East-Central European region are crucial in the formation of a variety of particular national complexes. Gombrowicz considers every national complex a hindrance to his artistic practice. "The writer, the artist, or anyone who attaches importance to his spiritual development, must feel no more than a resident in Poland or Argentine, and it is his duty to regard Poland or the Argentine as an obstacle, almost as an enemy. That is the way to feel really free" (*F,* 281). This psychopolitical complex forces the writer into borderline posturing. The patriotic small-mindedness is bound up with ridiculous identifications, with flag waving, with national anthems and legions of honor, and with habits that are imposed from the outside by an alienating culture. Polish identity is constantly threatened by a mixture of these foreign impositions, which gradually distort, dissolve, and soften it. "This feeling of formlessness tortured the Poles, but at the same time gave them a strange sense of liberty" (*F,* 278). This sense of liberty, originating in nonidentity, is what enables the borderline poetics to function in the political universe of Slavic culture. The fact that a sort of unsymbolized, demonic space still functions inside a culture can be a vital element for its transfiguration. It is a sign that the culture has not been thoroughly exhausted through the repetition of externally imposed religious forms and literary genres, but has been engendered in its abject, negative form, as a lack of proper identity. Gombrowicz's definition of Poland betrays a bitter realization that its national identity is necessarily bound to this negative metaphysics.

> It is a country between East and West, where Europe starts to draw to an end, a border country where the East and the West soften into each other. A country of weakened forms. . . . Those plains, open to every wind, had long been the scene of a great compromise between Form and its Degradation. Everything was effaced, disintegrated. . . . Poland, deprived of those great cities (and their bourgeoisie) where life can be concentrated and complicated, where it can arise and flourish, had a rural, peasant culture, yes, a culture represented by squires and priests. The nobleman sitting in his farmstead made the peasant do the work, and the village priest was the oracle. (*F,* 277)

This "peasant culture," defined as the source of regenerating

witold gombrowicz

immaturity, is one of the cultural reservoirs of Gombrowicz's novelistic poetics. In order to achieve existential authenticity, he hurls himself into this "immature" culture and posits youth as a value in itself, the only authentic posture granted him by Polish culture. He is not ready to bow down in front of the great centers of European antiquity and to produce a second-rate imitation of a great novel. He desires to become a European by unearthing the debilities of Polish culture and transforming them into his own poetic norms. In the process, he has to overcome the fear of impotence and feminization that the association with the lower classes and the inferior nations immediately invokes in the carriers of the ethnocentric European tradition. The writers who see themselves as the bearers of national culture, the embodiments of firm forms and masculinity, are actually afraid of the repressed layer of peasant culture and their own feminine qualities. Gombrowicz unmasks the fear of formlessness and peasant origins as disguised fear of being turned into something weak and feminine. "One could say that the spirit of this enhanced masculinity appeared in everything in history. I saw how this panic-stricken masculinity deprived such men not only of a sense of measure, but of all intuition in dealing with the world: where he needed to be flexible, he inflicted himself, pushing and flaying noisily with his whole being. Everything became excessive: heroism, severity, might, virtue."[13]

In order to avoid this masculine posturing of the modern hero, Gombrowicz first overcomes the fear of his own feminine dimension, his own Polishness, his own immaturity, and accepts them as something existent and therefore authentic. Only after accepting his own abject position can he proceed to deconstruct the models of the modern age and conceive of a borderline poetics, based on the admiration of that which is abominable.

beyond the limit

The task of casting out one's own masculinity is neither easy nor unambiguous and often results in explosions of misogyny. All the models of femininity, starting with the modern ideal embodied in

Miss Youthful and ending with Isabel, the timid country girl, are engendered through the defensive and aggressive posturing of the narrator. Johnny's encounters with the schoolgirl, who wears the mask of modernity with ease, and Isabel, the pale girl who belongs to the species found in dentists' waiting rooms, all point to his inability to give up his narcissism and identify with the woman he loves. Instead, Johnny is always caught up in master-slave relationships with them. He is totally subdued by the androgynous qualities of the athletic Miss Youthful, but this infatuation is involuntary, and he experiences it as a torture. Johnny fears that the modern girl's style will invade him and that he will have to spend the rest of his life imprisoned by the literary convention of unrequited admiration for her. The oral aggressive phantasies of his being "swallowed whole by a modern schoolgirl" betray an underlying fear of losing one's own proper identity and being engulfed by a more powerful entity.

At the same time, Gombrowicz reveals his secret wish to be desired like Miss Youthful. He envies her ability to seduce everyone with her perfect modern form, from the indifferent schoolboy Kopeida to that highest emanation of the superego—dreadful Professor Pimko. "Yes, if it happens that I despise women then it is because they are terrible priestesses of beauty and revealers of youth."[14] He feels that women are his most powerful opponents in the struggle for the enforcement of the aesthetic ideal, since beauty is their occupation and profession. It is through beauty that they deceive, like an artist who produces works of art in order to be loved. Gombrowicz is angered by their lack of aesthetic criteria and infuriated by their success in seducing men. The tone of his confession in the diary is charged with venom when he is forced to compare artistic practice with the feminine art of seduction: "I grow angry because they annoy and offend me as bad artists. Artists, yes, because charm is their vocation and aesthetics their profession."[15] He places women at the center of his invective because he feels that they have been given an unfair advantage as culturally constructed objects of desire. While he has to work hard in order to create works of art and become the center of attention, they occupy this position simply by virtue of being women. "They were born to fascinate, they are art to some extent themselves."[16] They are art, while he is just a maker of art. Unable to acknowledge that he himself wants to be a woman, Gombrowicz can only turn against her and ravage the foundation of her aesthetics. But, while he attacks women, he exposes the whole system of social and class roles that construct women as objects of aesthetic contemplation. He reprimands them for their "blindness and stupidity" when choosing a man, because they don't fall in love with the "Apollonian outlines of his body and soul."[17] Instead, they give themselves to "those men who are the embodiment of petty revulsion," the distinguished professionals who charm them with the "cheap pathos of an idiot."[18] Gombrowicz is angry at women for their lack of criteria, for their inability to distinguish between face and mask. "She does not know how to unmask, she allows herself to be deceived because she herself deceives."[19] This accusation originates in a feminine renunciation of a firm and recognizable identity, something that Gombrowicz strives after but has difficulty achieving. The art of feminine seduction is a product of the exclusion of women from political and social power structures; they are forced to use available means, transforming their bodies into aesthetic objects of male contemplation. This art of deception is the only weapon they are able to use in order to come closer to the power possessed by the patriarchs. Commenting on the behavior of the woman who slaps the face of her innocent neighbor because that is the only way she can discharge her rage, in the "Introduction to Philimor Honeycombed with Childishness," the narrator concludes that women allow themselves to act whimsically exactly because they have no power to do otherwise. "She did so because there was no other outlet for her indignation and because, in accordance with her essentially feminine logic, she felt (in the innermost depths of her unconscious) that, being a woman, everything was permitted her" (*F,* 194).

This "essentially feminine logic" is contemptible in Gombrowicz's view. Yet, he enforces exactly the same principles in his writing practice. He too would like to possess that freedom of the abject, who can do everything because they have nothing to lose. Woman is represented as a conceited being, out of touch with reality because of her aesthetic sublimation, so she can allow herself to act out her own frustrations without respect for others who may be innocent bystanders. The feminine rage, accumulated over centuries of oppression, finds its articulation in the modern age, which is the age of pseudo-matriarchal dictatorships that find support in the irrational appropriation of motherhood and femininity. This ideological construction has nothing to do with real, flesh-and-blood women, since the patriarchal power structure only appropriates images of womanhood in order to enforce its own "essentially feminine logic." "Here one must introduce an important distinction: it is not the woman that is terrible but today's femininity."[20] The situation in which women feel that everything is permitted creates a false sense of freedom, which is acted out in fashion and in the aestheticized art of deception. This permissiveness leads to the creation of styles and forms to which women conform while believing that they are exercising their freedom.

> What is awful is not the individual woman but the style that has arisen among women to which each woman succumbs. Who creates femininity? Men? Surely, man is the initiator, but afterward women themselves begin to perfect this among themselves and the art of misleading and enchanting, just like all others, grows and develops mechanically, automatically losing its sense of reality and sense of proportion. Today a woman is more of a woman than she should be: she is loaded with femininity, which is stronger than she is; she is the creation of a certain social convention, the consequence of a certain game, which pits man against woman until the dance grows and grows, becoming fatal.[21]

Gender roles are constructed by the unconscious operation of the "social convention," and the nature of the relationship between the sexes has been transformed into a battlefield of Gombrowicz's existential masks. These masks are designed by the binary oppositional logic of structuralism, which takes ascendance in European thought in the post–World War II period. The necessarily linguistic universe of the writer is split along the opposition of the body and language, the female and the male, the synthesis and the analysis. Unreality is Gombrowicz's weapon against the dictatorship of the binary structure. He cannot divide the imaginary wholeness of his own identity, but holds onto the primitive narcissistic logic of the desire for oneself. This borderline status sharpens his senses—he attempts transcendence

witold gombrowicz

by lowering himself into abjection and degradation, where the imperative for the new experience is still a possibility. ". . . I was aware that if I exchanged depression and apathy, wretchedness and poverty, for success, my power would vanish, for the truth was that it consisted of a magic superpower based on my avowed and acknowledged lack of it" (*F,* 141). The renunciation of power, indifference to external circumstances, is the condition of the borderline subject, enabling Gombrowicz to believe he can see through all the existential masks of humanity. The exhaustion of the middle-class ideals of both masculinity and femininity leads to excessive gender rituals that are repulsive to Gombrowicz, who loathes both sides of the socially constructed gender masks. "In order to prevent this, I had to find a different position for myself—beyond man and woman—which would nevertheless not have anything to do with a 'third sex'—an asexual and purely human position from which I could begin airing these stuffy and sexually flawed areas. So as not to be primarily a man, but a human being who just happens to be a man. Not to identify with masculinity, not to want it. If I could get out of this masculinity openly and decisively, its judgement of me would lose its bite and I could then say much about certain inexpressible things."22

Gombrowicz seeks disassociation from his gender, while envying women for the ease with which they can deceive from their marginalized position. He is also in search of an absolute aesthetics, of a style that could force the reader to swallow even the most outrageous phantasms from the author's unconscious. This betrays his secret desire to embody the knowledge of "certain inexpressible things," which lie on the other side of the commonplace notions of sexuality and morality. His imaginary desire for a "purely human position" that would loosen the chains of age, gender, and class determinants and place him in the realm of freedom, where the uttering of inexpressible things becomes possible, reveals the psychopolitical origins of his metaphysical longing.

The transcendental dimension, manifest both in Bulgakov's *The Master and Margarita* and in Gombrowicz's *Ferdydurke,* stems from the furious individualism of the marginalized writer, who is willing to break down the boundaries of conventional morality and hurl himself into the ordered abyss of language. The only sacred space left is the white page, which can be soiled with fictionalized confessions of the borderline writer. Language is the place where the writer can vent his torments and achieve the provisional identity created through the imaginary narratives of his novels. But while Bulgakov still prefers the veils of literary mystification and hides behind the identity of the Master, Gombrowicz is readier to admit that he is the only subject of his literary performances.

> The defence of my own personality. I knew what I had to write. I had to defend myself, to impose myself, to fight for myself! This new work had to serve me personally. And this was to be the guarantee of its being rooted in reality. Because, I thought, reality, this general, objective reality, is not reality at all. True reality is the one which is peculiar to you.
>
> I cannot write 'Tomato soup is good.' How misleading! But I am entitled to say 'I like tomato soup.' That's how we must talk! That's style. My work must become myself. (*F,* 273)

Rejecting the male position and scorning the female, Gombrowicz sees the narcissistic dimension of his own literary performance as the only weapon left against the tormenting unreality of "objective reality." The conspicuous egoism of his position is born from the author's defamiliarization of the rationalist posture.[23] Every discursive position is experienced as truthful, because Gombrowicz gives up all pretense to embody objectivity, but seeks to discover reality in the proclamation of universal subjectivity of his own rationality. In his case, the literary vision is fashioned through parodic posturing in the face of the superficial mannerisms of modern civilization. His first impulse is transcendental, but since transcendence is apparently naive and impossible, he has to shroud it in the disguise of pseudometaphysical parody.

Repulsed by the sexual masquerades of middle-class morality, Gombrowicz, the archpriest of immaturity, cynically postulates the human thigh as the mystical foundation of modern culture. "Their thighs would not leave them in peace. There was an irresoluble conflict between the thigh, unconscious and dormant in its primitive verdure, and all the things that the head dreamt about. But for that very reason there was never any reference to thighs, but a great deal about feelings, social or economic or society events, bridge, racing, and even about changing the structure of the state" (*F,* 154).

witold gombrowicz

The glorification of this partial object, which reads as a parody of Freud's insights into the realms beyond the pleasure principle, is the true cynical unmasking of the double standards of bourgeois morality. While in Miss Youthful's bedroom, Johnny conducts a search, which turns up "a pile of intimate letters from judges, lawyers, public prosecutors, chemists, businessmen, landlords, doctors, etc.," revealing the lusting of the feeble patriarchs after the perfection of the modern girl's athletic thigh (*F,* 157). They long to cast off the burdensome mask of maturity and savor this portion of her anatomy. But instead of openly expressing their desires, "the whole tribe of important, respectable people" writes letters to the modern girl and clothes its bodily needs in respectable outfits of social and economic programs (*F,* 157). Modern culture, founded on the vitality and dynamism of the youthful thigh, manages to subject the respectable adults to its irrational principles. "These letters revealed to me in a flash the extent of the power wielded by the modern girl" (*F,* 157). The old men of the twentieth century are yielding to the charms of a new aesthetics of modernism, which produces girls like Zutka. Her thigh is a symbol of the coming age of sexless athletic youths, who will wipe out the old world in the name of progress and hygiene. The Nietzschean ideal of the blond youth, standing above the morals of the servile rabble, finds its parodic expression in Miss Youthful, a Polish ridicule of the superman ideal. Gombrowicz finds Nietzsche's ideas completely wrong: "Why Nietzsche didn't have the least idea about these things, it is difficult to imagine something more tawdry, ridiculous, or in worse taste than his superman and his young human beast, no, it's not true, not completeness but inadequacy, worseness, inferiority, immaturity, are appropriate to that which is still young, i.e., alive."[24]

Miss Youthful's modern style shows how Poland perverts Nietzsche's amoral ideals. Modernity is a safeguard against the fear of "inadequacy, worseness, inferiority, immaturity," surviving in each of the respectful adults as a reservoir of shameful truths, which can always explode and destroy the mask of adulthood. But the superhuman mask of the adult is a direct product of a frightening compensation, substituting the falsity of human perfection and power for the truth of human inadequacy. This fact offends Gombrowicz's sense of "good taste" since it produces the ideological vision of superhuman power that leads to holocausts in the name of health, progress, and beauty. Johnny, the narrator of *Ferdydurke*, would rather live in the degradation of constant youth than in the falsity of adult identity. As he and Mientus leave the city in search of the stable-boy, Johnny notices how the people in the suburbs are being indoctrinated by the same ideology of modernism and progress that he had to swallow in the Youthful family. "There cabmen sang patriotic songs in chorus, producing a singularly naive effect; while yonder ex-farm-girls were being instructed in how to perceive the beauty of the setting sun; and dozens of idealists, doctrinaires, demagogues, and agitators formed up and reformed and deformed, disseminating their ideas, opinions, doctrines, views, all specially simplified and adapted for the use of simple people" (*F,* 199).

The dissemination and assimilation of ideologies, "all specially simplified and adapted for the use of simple people," stir up patriotic feelings and instruct in the perception of beauty in order to civilize the Polish peasant. Since peasants were always outside the historical and cultural mainstream, the high priests of pedagogy feel obliged to enlighten them by rooting out their backward rural habits. The product is the misbegotten citizen whose surface is urban, but whose behavior remains hopelessly unenlightened. The simplicity, ignorance, and degradation of the lower classes constitute advantages in the eyes of the disenchanted victims of enlightened pedagogy, Johnny and Mientus. As the two schoolboys leave the city, they mourn the destiny of the honest proletariat, who have been ridiculed by codes of behavior imposed on them by bourgeois culture. As Mientus observes the violence done to parts of their bodies, he exudes a deep sense of disappointment: "'Feet . . . in reality bare though shod—feet not meant for shoes, heads not meant for hats, peasant bodies with petty bourgeois embellishments. Nothing but face,' said Mientus, 'nothing sincere or natural, everything false, imitated and artificial. And not a stable-boy in sight!'" (*F,* 199).

Even when they step outside the city limits, the two adventurers are unable to find any face that is not grimacing until they reach the country estate of Johnny's Uncle Edward. This last episode of the novel is the focus for a particularly sharp analysis of the class structure of Polish society and the inevitability of revolutionary events, which are to take place in reality only a few years later. The peasants, transformed into dogs, bark at Johnny and Mientus in order to drive them away. Mientus, suddenly placed in the role of the city boy, tries to persuade the peasants that they don't need to bark, because he and Johnny have come from the city with a good intention: to find the genuine stable-boy. But the peasants prefer to be dogs and refuse to be changed into humans and citizens, a cultural form that the enlightened civilization has forced on the Polish lower classes. They speak in an uneducated manner, while resisting the two city boys.

> "Please, sorr, 'e be no stitizen, 'e be no stitizen, that's the last thing 'e be!" she pleaded. "Oh 'ow unlucky we be, 'ow unlucky! Here 'ey be, arter us again wi' 'eir intentions! . . .
>
> "'e wish us good!" his wife shrieked. "'e wish us good! We not 'umans, we dogs, dogs! Wuff! Wuff! . . . .
>
> "At 'em! At 'em! Bite the stitizen! Bite 'em and 'eir intentions!" they growled. (*F,* 203–04)

The peasants first pretend to be animals, acting out the role that has been imposed on them by their masters. The fear caused by civilization and its harmful benefits forces them to turn into abject, subhuman voices. But fear changes to aggression, which results in the attack of an old peasant woman who bites Johnny's belly. The "biting of intentions," the attack on the two parodic bearers of enlightenment, shows the degree of alienation of the serfs from the "human essence," which was so dear both to the Hegelians and to the Marxists. Feudal oppression has been so effective that the peasants have accepted the role that equates them with speaking cattle. The rustic stable-boy, whom Mientus finds in the person of the servant Bert, is an invention of pastoral literature, engraved in Mientus's mind as the incarnation of a pure being, living in complete harmony with nature. The animality of peasant aggression, produced by centuries of social and political oppression, is juxtaposed against the image that Mientus constructs as Bert's ideal identity. But Gombrowicz does not accept the world as a natural entity; he sees it as the constant staging of history and identity, which does not reveal the genuine nature of man and his world but produces a literary simulacrum.

The parody of nature and reality reaches its culmination toward the end of the novel when Gombrowicz transforms the sun into a giant human backside. "Meanwhile the super-bum mounted higher in the sky, sending out its dazzling rays by the million over a world which was a kind of imitation of the world, a paper world, painted green and illuminated from on high by blazing light" (F, 266). Haunted by the prevailing unreality of "a paper world" where personal identity is modeled after a literary convention, Johnny decides to run away from Uncle Edward's estate and abduct his unsuspecting daughter Isabel. He sees this as a possible affirmation of his manhood and maturity, something that will at least have the appearance of normality in the nightmarish world of feudal abnormality. "The normal is a tightrope over the abyss of the abnormal" (F, 251–52). So, instead of following Mientus's crazy idea of abducting the stable-boy and taking him to Warsaw with them as the perfect specimen of a face without a grimace, Johnny ends up with the equally absurd, but socially glorified idea of abducting Isabel. "Oh, the sensible and rational idea of abducting Isabel" (F, 252). Acting out the literary fantasy of a knight abducting a lady, Johnny escapes the latent homosexual desire of his alter ego for the imaginary innocence of the stable-boy. But the adventure with Isabel, who is "made for a dentist's waiting room," turns out to be just a repetition of a new set of social conventions that are predictable and artificial (F, 267). Her innocence and passivity irritate Johnny, who soon gets the urge to torture her. "Oh, to put some space between us, six inches at any rate, oh to refuse her, to get angry and strike her, to say something hostile to her, to be nasty, yes nasty to Isabel!" (F, 271). Thoroughly enchanted by the virility of Miss Youthful, Johnny shrinks at the thought of spending the rest of his days with a completely submissive Isabel. His identity is patterned along the lines of sadomasochistic psychopathology, with the initial grandiose expansion into the illusory realm of love and idealism, which is subsequently followed by the other phase of shrinking, regression, and explosion of identity, resulting in tension and suffocation. "The sense of growing, swelling, becoming huge, started all over again, lengthened and broadened, swelled and multiplied itself to the hundredth power, became tense, acute, stretched to bursting point, strain and tension, a sense of stifling monotony, tension, endless, boundless, infinite, a sense of submergence above and below . . ." (*F,* 256–57).

Gombrowicz tries to embody both existential positions at the same time, simultaneously feeling a sense of phallic exhilaration and suffocation, resulting from the abjection of those around him. Isabel provokes aggression because she embodies the quality of an eternal aunt who dulls the existential intensity Gombrowicz demands from the life of his characters. "There is nothing more splendid or more thrilling and intoxicating than that man gained a younger companion, who is at once a servant and a master."[25] This is the most revealing statement from the *Diary,* which explains Gombrowicz's favorite social and sexual game. The realm of the most intimate personal relationships is invaded by the Hegelian master-slave dialectic, where domination over and submission to a "younger companion" quickly become exhausted and boring. The other has to embody both roles at once, while the borderline subject holds onto its own narcissistic withdrawal from the games imposed by civilization. Gombrowicz envisions human relationships in terms of an endless reversal of the master-slave dialectic, which constantly challenges and undermines the notion of stable identity through excursions into the exotic regions of the subculture, dominated by marginal subjects: youths, women, peasants. "Nowhere could there be more concentrated exoticism, more fatal poisons, nowhere a more luxuriant blooming of phantasmagoria and rare flowers, nowhere else were these orchids and super-oriental butterflies to be found, no humming-bird from distant lands could compare in exoticism to a duck our hands had never touched" (*F,* 239–40).

The exotic and rare are to be found in the domain of the low and the inferior, which is at the same time the reservoir of originality and vitality of a particular culture. "A duck our hands had never touched" is a symbol of the other region that the dominant, serious culture ignores while pretending that it is promoting the values of the European centers of learning. In the process, the culture loses its vitality and suffers an inferiority complex. Woman, according to Gombrowicz, is another possible source of "that other voice," which can revitalize the Polish culture on its deathbed. "There is nothing more wondrous than the tone that a woman contributes, that other voice that is the mysterious completion of manhood, the conception of the world on another scale, a separate interpretation, inaccessible to me."[26] Although woman is constructed as a being of deception and is just "the mysterious completion of manhood," this statement certainly contradicts the general misogynist tone of Gombrowicz's writing.

By hurling himself into the abyss of subculture, where identity of the dominant class is not guaranteed, Gombrowicz paves the way for the liberation of small cultures from the oppression of the externally imposed aesthetic criteria. He is the prophet of cynicism who seeks the absolute border of identity that will transcend the socially imposed limits by descending into the realm of immaturity, perversion, and cruelty. The result is a parodic version of the existentialist paradox that is not resolved in the novel. Johnny ends up running away from Isabel, who is not an acceptable complementary force, and lamenting his destiny, which does not allow him to find a genuine identity. Concluding that "there is no shelter from face except in face," Johnny flees with his face in his hands (*F,* 272). Gombrowicz is certain that the only means of true liberation from the stifling provinciality of Poland lies in casting away all superimposed identities or masks. Only thus does he discover a borderline novelistic poetics based on the ability to resist ideology, which imposes cultural norms and falsifies his striving for authenticity. Gombrowicz precedes the existentialists, since he demonstrates that "authenticity" is just another myth, a posture assumed by the borderline identity that continues its search for "a purely human position." This quest for identity that can never be found in its absolute form is Gombrowicz's paradoxical answer to the riddle of human existence, an approach that favors the process of devolution over the grotesque masks that emerge from this endless search.

Danilo Kiš:

History, Performance, and Horror in *The Tomb for Boris Davidovich*

The Tomb for Boris Davidovich was published in former Yugoslavia in 1976.[1] Before its publication, Danilo Kiš was known to the literary public as one of the few innovators in the field of both Serbian and Yugoslavian prose. Burdened by the demands of realism with a specific national flavor, prose in Serbia obstinately rejected foreign literary influences as unauthentic and inappropriate to the specific historical and literary situation of Yugoslavia until the late twentieth century. This rejection was tacit and reflected the typical attitude of a provincial culture, which protects its own fragile identity from external "occupation" by defending its national character. This attitude, a

residue and a specific Yugo-hybrid of socialist realist doctrines, survived in Yugoslavia well into the 1970s. Literary practice, in the only
socialist country that withdrew from the Soviet bloc in 1948, is usually regarded as free from direct government censorship. But control
of the cultural scene is still maintained by "literary gangs" that use
rumor, character defamation, and sometimes threats in order to per-
petuate their rule over the literary Olympus in the Balkans. These
gangs have connections with those "very important personages" (of
the Gogolian type) in the higher government and Party echelons,
connections that give them almost limitless power in literary circles.

Kiš, a somewhat iconoclastic figure whose earlier books had introduced a variety of contemporary poetic practices, ranging from those
of Robbe-Grillet to that of Bruno Schulz, was a thorn in the sides of
those purist guardians of the national literature. For Belgrade's literary gangsters, *The Tomb for Boris Davidovich* was just too much.
Since the book used a variety of intertextual techniques and explicitly
borrowed from other texts (Kiš provided an extensive bibliography),
the literary Mafia accused him of plagiarism. The result was the
greatest postwar literary scandal and polemic in Yugoslavia, which
luckily ended in a triumph for Kiš and his defenders. This marked a
turning point in the further development of Yugoslavian, and particularly Serbian, prose, which broke with the narrow canons of realism
and started exploring new forms and themes, inspiring the next generation of Yugoslavian prosaists.

The entire polemic focuses on the question of plagiarism and literary originality, an issue frequently raised in the context of national
literatures that adopt the romantic notion of pristine originality,
which amounts to "reading Njegoš, the epic poetry and listening to
the tales of your grandmother."[2] Kiš made a point of borrowing from
other texts, consciously adopting the Borgesian poetics of pseudohis-
toricity. By blending the actual documents with the apocryphal ones,
he created a fictional world that offered a more powerful political
denunciation of totalitarianism than many historical or historiographic texts. In the opening chapter of *The Tomb of Boris Davidovich*,
entitled "The Knife with a Rosewood Handle," the narrator explains
that his aim is to achieve a universal language of horror, a task that he

necessarily fails to accomplish. The book is an attempt to reinvent the
"terrifying moment of Babel" that is present in the post-revolutionary
reality of East-Central Europe (*TBD*, 5). The novel is written from
the perspective of the victims of this totalitarian project and summed
up in the destiny of a Jewish woman whose death rattle is the
symbolic expression of the new Babel, engendered within the
Communist world. "If the narrator, therefore, could reach the
unattainable, terrifying moment of Babel, the humble pleadings of
Hanna Krzyzewska would resound in Romanian, in Polish, in
Ukrainian (as if her death were only the consequence of some great
and fatal misunderstanding), and then just before the death rattle
and final calm her incoherence would turn into the prayer for the
dead, spoken in Hebrew, the language of being and dying"(*TBD*, 5).

Most of the protagonists in the book are Jews or of Jewish origin,
like Kiš himself, which makes the problem of the new Babel even
more interesting. The mythical punishment by God is the confusion
of tongues that follows Babel and reaches culmination in the twentieth century when the reconstruction of the new tower is attempted
by the Comintern. The international brotherhood of Communists,
by adopting Russian as its universal language in the 1930s, attempts
to build the new Babel by denying the divine authority of religion
and seizing absolute power over the material realm. Kiš reverses the
metaphor of the universal language to show the resulting horrors,
which are usually "the consequence of some great and fatal misunderstanding" (*TBD*, 5).

The adoption of a Borgesian pseudohistorical poetics allows Kiš to
deconstruct the new Babel, to show the absurdities and discontinu-
ities in the attempt of totalitarian ideologists to attain their proclaimed goals of universal peace and brotherhood on the planet. In
order to present his counter-ideology and to demonstrate the highly
fragmented nature of this new reality, Kiš chooses a borderline literary genre. *The Tomb for Boris Davidovich* is subtitled "Seven Chapters
of the Same Narrative," which apparently places it between a collection of short stories and a novel. But since the unifying subtext is
implicit in the individual stories of the protagonists, whose destinies
are always directed by the same cruel force of revolutionary history, I

will treat *The Tomb for Boris Davidovich* as a novel, adopting Kundera's broad definition of the genre.[3] One of the reasons writers from this borderline region use a fragmented novelistic structure to articulate their existential positions is their apparent feeling of suspicion of any form of monological, unified narration. The strategies employed in these works use fragmentation, nonlinear narration, and blending of fact and fiction to undermine the language and culture of totality enforced by the state and the Party. These two institutions have abused the privileged position of monolithic power for too long, falsifying their subjects' sense of a stable and reliable reality by the vulgar perversions of Marxist thought. The "variation on a theme" model of the novel is a response from the writer who rejects the imperatives of a literary realism, tainted by this aspect of totalitarian ideology.

the destruction of ethics

The individual chapters of *The Tomb for Boris Davidovich* insist on telling the same story about the tragic destiny of the European and Russian intellectuals whose leftist ideals are eroded after their destructive confrontation with the bureaucracy of the Comintern. Kiš was attacked by the Belgrade literary establishment (or "literary government," as he calls it) because he refused to dissimulate, to pretend that the revolutionary history of international communism was a glorious political project, and to ignore the massive bloodshed and the imprisonment and intimidation of those who dared to be individuals and to think differently. The protagonists of *The Tomb for Boris Davidovich* are all convinced revolutionaries whose destinies at a certain moment fall under the control of a force larger than themselves. They are never made fully aware of their guilt or crime, and most of them (like Kafka's Joseph K.) spend their time in prison cells and labor camps, meditating on the nature and cause of their transgressions. The blind force of the historical process turns them into helpless automatons, subhuman entities who struggle to rationalize their lives and to discover the meaning of existence in suffering for

the cause of the revolution. Almost invariably, they give in to the
pressure of their inquisitors and make false confessions, assuring
themselves a place in the larger historical process as gruesome fertil-
izer of the proverbial revolutionary struggle that favors those who are
determined to use all means to retain and defend their class position.

Interrogator Fedukin, the master of prison psychology, wishes to
justify the revolutionary process by extracting false confessions from
political prisoners. Even Boris Davidovich Novsky himself succumbs
to the methods of the demonic policeman. But Novsky's ethical trials
aside, it is Fedukin who reveals to the reader the true motivation of
the revolutionary bureaucracy. We are told that Novsky had represented for Fedukin a revolutionary ideal and that the interrogator is
bitterly disappointed when the prisoner refuses to sign the confession, which has already been written for him by the interrogator. He
is annoyed because "Novsky could not understand that his own egocentricity (surely a product of flattery and praise) is stronger in him
than his sense of duty" (*TBD*, 99). Fedukin's notion of the mythical
revolutionary who is never troubled by trivial technicalities regarding
truth or the meaning of individuality when his "historical mission" is
at stake is severely shaken by Novsky's refusal to sign the confession.
Although Fedukin is aware that the confession is unrelated to
Novsky's real deeds, he expects the true revolutionary to sacrifice his
"egocentricity" and sign the false confession if authorities demand
that he do so. "Fedukin knew just as well as Novsky (and let him
know it) that all this—the entire text of the confession, formulated
on ten single-spaced pages—was pure fiction, which he alone,
Fedukin, had concocted during the long hours of the night, typing
with two fingers, awkwardly and slowly (he liked to do everything
himself), trying to draw logical conclusions for certain assumptions"
(*TBD*, 98).

This larger truth of the historical process is constructed by the real
engineers of the human soul, the professional revolutionary bureau-
crats, whose monstrous depreciation of individual human lives lead
to the massive purges of the entire Communist movement in the
thirties. Fedukin, the sadistic interrogator, whose "undeniable literary
talent" contributes to the fictional quality of Novsky's confession,

represents the most extreme example of Arendt's concept of the banality of evil (*TBD*, 91).[4] Torturers and criminals are also good fathers or persons capable of creating art and contemplating beauty of nature. But once he realizes that the direct torture of Boris Davidovich Novsky will not yield any positive results, he orders the guards to murder a young man each day in front of the prisoner. Like a specialist in Pavlovian conditioning, before the young man is shot he repeats the sentence: "If Novsky doesn't confess, we'll kill you" (*TBD*, 93). The words are spoken to the young man, but are really intended to undermine Novsky's moral resolve. With the cold-blooded detachment of a scientist, the investigator observes the changes in the prisoner's face as he watches the young man, dead in a pool of blood. The monstrosity of the police genius, who stands above humanist morality, manages to break down Novsky, who is determined to end his life as an honest revolutionary, sacrificing the temporality of his own existence for the eternal glory of history. The suffering and death of innocent prisoners, slaughtered by Fedukin because of Novsky's obstinacy, finally breaks through the latter's impenetrable armor and awakens his emotions. "Behind his tightly shut lids there arose in him, simultaneously with the reawakening of pain and the premonition of failure, hatred; he had enough time to realize that Fedukin had seen through him and had decided to devastate him where he felt the strongest: in his egocentricity" (*TBD*, 93).

The awakening of ethics in Boris Davidovich Novsky, as he is sacrificed to the irrational demands of the monolithic ideology of Stalinism, proves the interrogator's point that the individual cannot exist only by the rules created by his own "egocentricity." Paradoxically, Fedukin teaches Novsky the lesson of collective responsibility to the higher demands of ideology: by murdering innocent prisoners to show Novsky that his obstinacy will only contribute to the annihilation of others, Fedukin forces him to lie and to accept his fictional guilt in order to save other prisoners. And although Novsky wishes to endure to the end the torture that is turning him into an "empty shell of being," the moral imperative to deny truth in order to save others is stronger than his desire for canonized status in the gallery of Bolshevik saints (*TBD*, 92).

Kiš demonstrates that the individual becomes obsolete as an ethical and existential entity after the Communist revolution. The only thing that matters is the place of that individual in the larger revolutionary plan, a name or number in a government register. Human life is devalued and debased, reduced to the level of a token in a revolutionary gamble, where people are shifted about by those who are in a position to replace the authority of the Christian God and to determine the outcome of human lives. In a chapter entitled "The Magic Card Dealing," Kiš presents a treatise on the games of chance that affect the life of a Gulag prisoner (*TBD*, 53). While the narrator recounts the events that lead to the death of another revolutionary idealist, Dr. Taube, the reader learns about the social hierarchy in the Gulag. The ruling class is made up of the true criminals, who are regarded as "socially acceptable" by the prison authorities since they inevitably oppose the class of pre-1917 masters. Those who are accepted into the Party ranks after a life of crime are always more reliable in the eyes of the camp administration because their class position makes them ideal allies of the Communists. "Millions of political prisoners were exposed to all the whims and idiosyncrasies of this group, the so-called socially acceptable" (*TBD*, 54). For Kiš, the historical experience of the Gulag represents a reversal of values, marking the end of the humanist age. The reversal caused by the revolutionary inversion of social values favors the manipulative criminal over the idealistic intellectual. The unleashed, animalistic power of the criminal mind destroys the codes of humanist ethics derived from the Judeo-Christian moral imperatives. Respect for individual life is replaced by the improbable code of criminal morality, which is given the sign of the devil. "The Devil or the Mother represents a whole symbolic coded language very similar to the Marseilles Tarot. It is interesting, however, that the hardened criminals, those with longer prison experience, used the handmade cards for another kind of communication: often, instead of using words, they would pick up a card and suddenly, as if by an order, a knife would flash, blood would spill" (*TBD*, 64).

It is symptomatic that the top two criminals who play the game of "The Devil or The Mother" are given animal names—Monkey and

Eagle. The notions of spirit, mind, and soul are destroyed by the demonic reappearance of the animalistic body in its aggressive posture. The inmates of the Gulag are ruled by the destructive game of chance, which is an allegory for the entire structure of revolutionary society. The new language of symbolic gestures represents a code of honor and justice that is understood only by the initiated criminals. The old system of values is officially abolished and replaced by a new, Darwinian-Marxist vision of man. The Party decides who is an active passenger on the ship of history and who is a superfluous burden. This new code, based on physical strength and political abjection, negates the humanist foundations of Western civilization. Humans are turned into exhausted predators who satisfy their symbolic urges by playing with the lives of other humans. The loser in the game that bears the name of "The Devil or the Mother" (the direct opposite of the game of Christianity played by God and the Father) kills the one named by the winner. The victim of the game in Kiš's story is Dr. Taube, a Hungarian revolutionary idealist who finds himself inexplicably in prison. The power structure and its regulatory mechanisms, like the language of the criminals, are opaque and mysterious to the political prisoners in the Gulag. The categories of good and evil are reversed, since the revolution erases the borderline separating them and replaces it with an instrumental code of conduct for the control of its subjects. "And that was all they knew, all they could possibly know; except for this horrendous language of silence and curses, the political prisoners were altogether unfamiliar with the coded speech of criminals, and the words whose meaning they did know were of no help anyway because in thieves' slang the meanings have shifted: God means the devil and the devil means God" (*TBD*, 68).

The literary characters in Kiš's story suffer from what Deleuze and Guattari have called "the Kafka effect."[5] The human beings are fueled by the undigested ideology, which transmutes them into biological machines who accept their punishment as an inevitable condition of existence and thus validate the laws of the new society inside the concentration camp. The uncanny alliance between the criminals and the Gulag masters lays bare the foundation of the revolutionary reversal of values. The criminals identify with the prison authorities and eradicate the revolutionary intellectuals, who threaten the order based on irrationality and obedience precisely because they are capable of rational thought. Kiš's reference to the "horrendous language of silence and curses" is an implicit critique of the futurists and their insistence on the trans-rationality of the poetic language: the criminals are already communicating in a realm beyond articulated speech, an unpredictable consequence of the avant-gardist dream. The language of the criminals is capable of "defamiliarizing" common, pre-revolutionary meanings to the extent that it can turn them into their opposites, the end result of the futurist project: "God means the devil and the devil means God."

The bureaucratic machinery that erases the foundation of humanist ethics is foregrounded in Kiš's work as the only winner of the magic card dealing game that the criminals play in the Gulag. After Gogol, Dostoyevski, and Kafka, Kiš gives another, almost occult interpretation of the ways in which bureaucracy corrupts, destroys, and censors individuals and their personal ethical standards. The destruction of ethical standards is the most acute point of the Kiš critique of totalitarian ideology. Both the commissar and the criminal have common class enemies: priests, landowners, and merchants, who have imposed upon the old world the values of the old God and his commandments. After the revolution, the ideologists promise, the old values will be eradicated and replaced by new ones based on the labor of the unalienated working class, which will build the new world according to the principles of science and technology. But the structure of the Gulag shows that the revolution only substitutes and reverses the symbolic codes, while the hierarchy of class society becomes even more pronounced. The workers are oppressed again, except that now the revolutionary bureaucracy rules in their name, and not in the name of God or the Tsar.

Good and evil lose their meaning in this context; at the same time, the individual is forced to decide whether something is instrumental to his physical survival or not. The police bureaucracy manufactures enemies of the people like a factory fulfills its five-year plan. Boris Davidovich is a notable exception here: he struggles against his investigator to assure his place in history, not to survive physically.

danilo kiš

Fedukin, a contemporary version of Dostoyevski's Grand Inquisitor, forces Boris Davidovich to forget about the historical figure he might cut and admit to false charges. The investigator embodies the principle that governs the Soviet revolution: production must be in accordance with a central plan, even if it requires the falsification of products. If someone is cast in the role of enemy of the people, he has to act in accordance with the plot. Miksha, the protagonist of the "Knife with a Rosewood Handle" chapter, reacts in a more typical way when confronted with his charges. When he is accused of the murder of Hanna Krzyzewska, he confesses not only to that crime (committed in accordance with his Party duties) but also to crimes he invents in order to become a more dynamic part of the central plan. "After months of starvation, beating, and torture, this was a bright moment in Miksha's life, this warm and pleasant office, where an old Russian stove crackled as one had long ago in Miksha's house in Bukovina, this tranquility beyond the muffled blows and the shrieks of prisoners, this portrait that smiled at him so like a father. In sudden rapture of faith, Miksha wrote down his confession: that he was an agent of the Gestapo, that he had worked to sabotage the Soviet government" (*TBD*, 14–15).

Miksha is a model prisoner: he falls in love with those who are torturing him and is inspired by a "rapture of faith" that enables him to make a false confession and believe in it. Stalin, smiling from a picture on the wall, gives him the necessary confidence to list twelve invented accomplices in the imaginary sabotage that they have planned together. In the nostalgic atmosphere of the interrogator's office, Miksha finally understands that if the authorities want him to play the role of the enemy in the theater of history, he has to play it so well that the role will become reality. In the process, the true murder of Hanna Krzyzewska fades into the background and becomes less important then the fictitious sabotage, which fits better into the central plot of the revolutionary theater.

Each of the protagonists of *The Tomb for Boris Davidovich* is moved by a force that he can neither control nor contain. This force, which manifests itself in the history of the revolutionary movement, is bent on destroying everything that opposes or shows signs of differing from it. Kiš presents this force as a game of chance, which creates a world where nothing is founded on rationality and morality, but only on misfortune and cruelty. Dr. Taube becomes a stake in the prisoner's game of "The Devil or the Mother" because he saves the fingers of Segidulin, the inmate who wins in the game. Segidulin hates Dr. Taube for saving his fingers because that obliges Segidulin to continue hard labor in the camp. The moral dilemma becomes obvious: the doctor tries to save a man who does not want to be saved and who, therefore, does everything to have the doctor killed. The foundations of Western rationality are challenged by the Gulag system, since in this inverted system of values it is better to be crippled or dead than it is to be healthy and, even worse, able to work. Boris Davidovich chooses death over life many times, but his investigator knows that there are worse things than dying. Although Boris Davidovich pleads for a death sentence in front of a firing squad, the court sentences him to labor camp and exile. He becomes mentally unstable, has auditory hallucinations, and tries to escape many times from the prison camp. He finally manages to die by jumping into a furnace of molten metal to escape his pursuers. Even death itself is good and desirable when compared with the horrors of life in the camp.

But for Kostik Korshunidze, the criminal who loses the game and kills Dr. Taube, the Gulag is a natural environment, much better than life on the other side. "Incidentally, Kostik thought of his prison term as an inseparable part of his work, just as former revolutionaries regarded theirs as 'universities'" (*TBD*, 54). This comparison strengthens the tie between the criminal and the bureaucrat, since they rely equally on the destruction of the previous political system. The narrator claims that prison was for Kostik, "as for so many thieves of all kinds, only an extension of 'freedom'" (*TBD*, 54). Kostik's last name, like Stalin's (Džugašvili), betrays a Georgian origin, an intentional similarity. By transposing the two characters, Kiš presents the Gulag as a microcosm and "an extension of the whole Soviet society," where the charismatic leader is followed by "whole legions of hardened criminals submitted to his will" (*TBD*, 54).

The historical turmoil caused by the revolution leaves a moral vacuum, a situation that favors those who believe that everything is permitted them. The destruction of the metaphysical foundation of morality that follows the "death of God" forces the participants of history to create their own moral codes. Kostik blindly carries out the murder of Dr. Taube after he loses the game of cards with another prisoner in order to show his almost religious faith in the new code. By murdering Dr. Taube, Kostik obeys the basic mechanism of political dealing, the agreement between the two powers, even if it means death and destruction of other human beings who are without the power to decide anything. The "magic card dealing" determines the destiny of Dr. Taube, who has neither the knowledge to understand nor the power to prevent his own death.

Kiš attacks the basic principle of the "old world order" that has directed the destiny of entire nations from the end of the Second World War until 1989. Like the criminals playing cards in the abject world of the Gulag, Stalin, Churchill, and Roosevelt decided the destiny of the world at Yalta, using human lives as bargaining chips. This infernal game of war and destiny transforms the course of Western history by eliminating Hitler's plan of a world empire. But the winners usually take everything that losers leave on the table. The entire planet is divided into spheres of influence. Stalin is given domination over the entire Slavic population on the planet, plus a few other non-Slavic East-Central European nations. Kiš objects to this, identifying himself with the victims, with the peoples who were devoured by the Soviet Empire in this terrifying game of chance, where the criminals are disguised as politicians.

history as performance

The borderline identity, or lack of a stable identity, is created in Kiš's prose through the ultimate revolutionary fragmentation of humanist ethics. Motivation is no longer dependent on moral choices but on the process of natural selection, with the application of Spencer's social doctrines in a literal, Darwinian manner: those who approximate the cruelty of the predator are the fittest and will survive the purgatory of the revolutionary struggle. The lower classes, which have managed to endure the process of dehumanization by their feudal and bourgeois masters for centuries, are now placed in the position of the rulers. The only power that can contain their brute force is the system of oppression founded on Stalinist falsification of Marxism. The Communists play the leading role in this new religion, like an inner circle of initiates who point the way for the uneducated masses. They preach that the true Communist always sets his personal views aside and behaves like a good soldier, carrying out orders with conviction and confidence. On the other hand, the Communist stands morally above those who do not belong to the Party and is justified even when he kills, robs, and lies—provided he is acting in the service of the revolutionary struggle. Although this type of "correct behavior" is not always a guarantee of survival, it is the only way tacitly posited by the new totalitarian system.

The priest is replaced by the commissar, a prototype of the new anthropological category that the Soviet political system produces in the 1930s. Kiš parodically demonstrates how the commissar sometimes has to revert back to the role of the priest in order to successfully perform his Party duty. Chelyustnikov, an amateur actor with good Party standing, is the best example of a bureaucrat who uses his acting skills in order to simulate reality. In the chapter "Mechanical Lions," the Kiev Party Committee decides to make use of Chelyustnikov's acting experience in order to dupe the left-wing French official Herriot, who comes to Kiev to verify whether the rumors about religious prosecution in the Soviet Union are true. The officials plan the performance in the famous Kiev church of Saint Sophia, which has been converted into a brewery after the revolution. "The constant temperature of 50° Fahrenheit is particularly suitable for the growth of those useful bacteria that give beer its unique taste" (*TBD*, 40). The narrator's sarcastic comment on the suitability of the cathedral for the fermentation of beer shows the extent to which appreciation of artistic and historical monuments has collapsed. The frescoes and icons are covered with a long hemp curtain and, instead of the Immaculate Virgin, there stands a portrait of the "Father of the People." The symbols of power have been changed, and the church now produces beer for the working class instead of "opiate for the people."

The brewery is quickly reconverted into a church for the sake of a foreign visitor, with Chelyustnikov playing the part of the priest. The cunning with which the cynical commissars cheat their French sympathizer shows the status of truth within the new totalitarian society. Truth is always a production, a necessary lie, instrumental in the achievement of a political aim. Kiš pictures historical events as performances, performances imagined and staged by the same unpredictable force that guides the game of "Devil or the Mother." The ugly underside of ideology (which pretends to preach love and equality) is inherent in every massive and violent attempt to modify the human mind and change the course of history. Kiš exposes totalitarian logic in a specific historical context, employing a historiographic tone and documentation to record the grotesque political reality created by Stalinism. "History does not invent, it discovers," writes Milan Kundera discussing the poetics of Jan Skacel.[6] Kiš adopts a similar poetic credo, posing as the infernal archivist whose utterances are based on research of the historical or pseudo-historical documents. The narrator of *The Tomb for Boris Davidovich* is caught up in a very difficult situation, since the method of literary discovery approximates the rewriting of history, which is often practiced by the official ideologists. But since Kiš takes the side of the victims to challenge the official history, the reader is more likely to accept his version of events as the one reflecting the true suffering of the protagonists. However, the narrative account of events (the source of both fiction and history) is a problematic and dangerous activity, since it represents the truth in a linear, non-problematic manner. Kiš recognizes this and comments on the narrator's "inability to forgo the pleasure of narration" because he may succumb to "the deceptive idea that he is creating the world and thereby, as they say, changing it" (*TBD*, 30). The author who lives under the constant surveillance of the commissars is aware that he cannot afford to delude himself in such a way. He knows it is the ideologists who are creating and changing the world by manipulating language and historical fact. The task of the writer is to expose ideologists to show the contradictions inherent in linearity and monologism, and to construct an alternative history that will make no promises, nor claim absolutely to represent reality. In "Mechanical Lions," the performance of history designed for the unfortunate Herriot starts as soon as he arrives at the local railway station. "Comrade Pyasnikov demanded that the poster with the slogan RELIGION IS THE OPIATE OF THE PEOPLE be removed and promptly replaced by another with a somewhat more metaphysical sound: LONG LIVE THE SUN, DOWN WITH THE NIGHT" (*TBD*, 36).

The slogan is replaced by Pushkin's verse that has "a more metaphysical sound" in order to deceive the naive Frenchmen, but also to manifest the falsity of the Communist Enlightenment, which is conveyed through ideological advertising of the most vulgar kind. The fundamental error of the ideologist lies in his striving to put himself in the position of the creator of the new order who blends pagan symbolism with the desire for "light." The commissars are given the power to decide about the destiny of others, assuming the role that was occupied by the Christian God before the revolution. This new coding is easily transposed into the field of the revolutionary-reactionary opposition, with every political deviation from the norm labeled as belonging to the night, darkness, and backwardness, reactionary tendencies that should be overcome by any means available. The glorification of the sun and its light contrasts sharply with the dark reality of the deeds of the commissars, a mythic subtext whose contradictions are examined in *The Tomb for Boris Davidovich*.

Under the direction of his political boss Pyasnikov, Chelyustnikov plays the leading role in the historical performance acted out for Herriot's benefit. He is told to disguise himself as an Orthodox priest, and he takes advantage of this opportunity to observe the reaction of the Russian people to the officially scorned clergy. When his driver does not recognize him and kisses his hand, Chelyustnikov comments in his report, not without disappointment, that "there is no limit to human credulity" (*TBD*, 44). He is disgusted by the reverence the common folk shows for his beard and the cross, concluding that "it will take a great deal of time and effort before all traces of the dark past are weeded out of the peasants' soul" (*TBD*, 44). The past is dark, the future is bright. The past should be erased and forgotten, religion should be eliminated by denial and eradication and replaced by a striving for the absolute brightness promised by science and technology. But the commissars are just repeating the historical pattern: like the Christian missionaries who fought to exterminate pagan beliefs in Russia, the Communists also try to "weed out the dark past" of Christian domination from the souls of peasantry. The people, in whose name the revolution is carried out, are constantly subjected to the reversals of ideologies, which are supposed to provide them with a "better future" whether in this world (under the ideology of communism) or in the other (under the ideology of Christianity). Belief in a "better future" is used as a tool of deception by the Holy Bureaucracy, which replaces the Christian Trinity with the trinity of Party, Army, and Police. The entire course of history is interpreted as a theatrical role playing of the revolutionary victims, with only the times, places, and names of the protagonists changing. The course of history is directed by the unconscious ideological performance of the same roles, the only roles available in a model founded on the strict polarization of cultural opposites. In the end, everyone is a loser. Even Chelyustnikov, who receives a medal for his role in the Herriot deception, is later sent to the camps for his own sins against the revolution. The night before his appearance on the stage, he has a dream that confirms the performative nature of history. "Terrified (in the dream), he heard the bell calling him to the stage, but he stood as if petrified, or, rather, sat, naked and hairy, unable to move. Suddenly, as if all this was happening onstage, the curtain rose, and through the dazzling side lights, which held him in the cross fire of their rays, he made out the audience, up in the balcony and down in the orchestra, their heads illuminated by purple haloes" (*TBD*, 32).

This parodic version of the emperor's new clothes manifests the symptomatic fear of the borderline personality, who is forced constantly to play different roles and is unable to achieve a real and stable identity. This is political pathology rather than psychopathology. The subject is part of a political experiment, where the notion of reality is dictated by the Central Plan, which, like a dramatic plot, establishes socially acceptable scenarios. While in Comrade M.'s house, Chelyustnikov is resting and dreaming after an adulterous encounter with M.'s wife when the phone rings and evokes the ringing of the stage bell in his dream. He is already in the act of moral transgression when "they" call him, making him aware that he cannot keep any secret from "them." The comrades from the Provincial Committee are calling on him to perform his historical duty and use his acting skills to produce a false version of reality. His dream reveals that "they" are identical to the omnipotent entities that haunt the imagination of the paranoid. "They" even penetrate his dream while he stands before them without any disguise, literally naked on stage. Chelyustnikov is called onto the historical stage and has to act for those whose heads are "illuminated with purple haloes." The new, cruel saints, directed by Pyasnikov, are demanding that he get up (although it is past midnight) and report to them immediately. Their power borders on the supernatural. Chelyustnikov has to obey, since his personal will is erased by the Party machinery. He is only the player, the subject who acts only as directed by those in charge of the show. This ludic, theatrical aspect of the revolution manifests the extent to which the "objectivity of the historical process" can be directed, falsified, and rewritten like a play. The Comintern creates the roles and hands the actors their stage directions. It pretends to act in the interest of the people by outlawing every deviation from its own ideology. The Marxist method of dialectical materialism becomes the tool of hypocrisy in a totalitarian system of social control by enabling the ideologist to disguise himself behind the old/new dichotomies. And behind these dichotomies, there is only one voice, commanding the millions of oppressed people, who, like Chelyustnikov, obediently act out their historical roles, afraid to offend the bureaucratic machinery that can eliminate them with the power of a merciless god.

The destiny of the protagonists illustrates the monological nature of the Party's performance. Both Novsky and Dr. Taube, like Kafka's K., are accused without an apparent or logical cause. Chelyustnikov is sent to the camp because Comrade M. wants to settle his private scores with him. The charge is based on the fact that "for three years he was the lover of the wife of an extremely prominent person (and for precisely that reason was sent to a labour camp)" (*TBD*, 31).

danilo kiš

Although he successfully performs his part in the Herriot affair, Chelyustnikov nevertheless ends up in the Gulag. The Party does not grant security even to those who appear to be ideologically correct, like Chelyustnikov. Unlike Bakhtin's happy relativity of a carnival, the post-revolutionary reality is characterized by an unhappy instability, enforced by the return of the same demonic presence under a different ideological mask. This historical theater of cruelty, whose repertoire Kiš borrows from the Borgesian concept of the Great Lottery, is propelled by the "incarnate principle of a mythical and evil deity" (*TBD*, 63).

Kiš's heroes move in a universe of uncanny silence that is interrupted only by the sounds of the victims' death rattle. Silence, if used correctly, can also have a lasting dramatic effect on a borderline personality, who is cast in the world of fear and confusion. Darmolatov, the hero of the last chapter, becomes so paranoid after a silent phone call (following the arrest of his protector, Novsky) that "he washed his hands in methyl alcohol and saw an informer in everyone" (*TBD*, 134). Darmolatov's example is used to demonstrate how far the Party machinery will go in subduing intellectuals. "They say that in relatively lean times Novsky was his 'connection'—a word indicating the complex bond between poets and the government whereby, on the basis of personal sympathies and sentimental debts of youth, the rigidity of the revolutionary line was softened. (Such a bond was greatly entangled and full of danger: if the powerful protector fell into disfavor, all the protégés rolled down the steep hill after him, as if carried by lava set in motion by the scream of the unlucky one.)" (*TBD*, 132).

When the phone rings in Darmolatov's apartment and he hears only silence on the other end of the line the paranoid mechanism is set in motion. Darmolatov packs his suitcases, ready to enter the Gulag and play the guilty role if it is assigned to him by "them." The punishment never comes, since "they" probably know that he has internalized the oppressor and is performing all the necessary operations himself. Darmolatov becomes even more paranoid and hallucinates informers and agents everywhere. "They persistently visited him, unannounced and without knocking, wearing colorful cravats, like lovers of poetry, or like translators, bringing miniature Eiffel Towers made of gold tin, or like plumbers, with enormous guns in their back pockets instead of plungers" (*TBD*, 134). Darmolatov's paranoia is comical, although the humor comes in moments of the most horrible abjection or madness. His fear of the silent and invisible force paralyzes the affirmation of his personality, leaving him in an anxious void, populated by "the colorful cravats of poets" and "the miniature Eiffel Towers of translators," the kitschy ornaments used by the secret police to hide their listening devices. There is, thus, no need for the police to do anything other then call and be silent. The silence acts as a screen onto which Darmolatov projects all of his secret anxieties, inventing the paranoid scenario and behaving exactly the way police want him to. Paradoxically, his paranoia is, in fact, the most adequate response to the political situation of the 1930s. Himself a mediocre poet, Darmolatov lives in a world where Akhmatova, Gumilev, Mandelstam, and others are arrested, persecuted, and marginalized during the purges. Darmolatov does not threaten the state in any way, but nevertheless he feels guilty, since the dissolution of ethical standards leaves him in a horrible vacuum where everyone is guilty and everyone is a potential enemy.

The historical theater of cruelty is organized around "an enlarged metaphor of the Great Lottery in which winning is rare and losing the rule" (*TBD*, 63). The protagonists are thrown onstage as "the victims of this inexorable merry-go-round, driven by the spirit of an at once platonic and infernal *imitatio*" (*TBD*, 63). The revolution creates a universe of uncertainty, where the reeling circulation of human destinies is governed by the pretense and simulation of ideology. The interrogator and the commissar act like gods, as do Kostik and Segidulin, the criminal lords of the Gulag, in an infinite circulation of unstable, borderline identities. Their ideals are "at once platonic and infernal" because the Party aspires to the divine heights of ideology while using the methods of the amoral depths of power. This arbitrary, repetitive nature of human history is the revelation around which Kiš organizes the documentary material of his novel: "all this suddenly appeared in my consciousness as an enlarged metaphor of the classical doctrine of the cyclic movement of time"

danilo kiš

(*TBD*, 124). The protagonists are moved by the temporal pattern of repetition that is not apparent in history, by the law of circular meaning that characterizes all despotic, pre-Christian temporal organizations. "In this context the sequence of *variability* is without great significance" (*TBD*, 125). Kiš's novelistic poetics is concerned with this insignificant "sequence of variabilities" that oscillates according to the same, suprahistorical laws of destiny and cruelty. The protagonists are actors in a play of interchangeable identities, in a gruesome scenario performed behind the opaque veil of totalitarian ideology. The idea of the cyclical historical recurrence of the infernal *imitatio* is present on all narrative levels of the novel.

The French official Herriot's analysis of the events in Kiev betrays that Russia was the scene of similar circus-like performances of power in the past. "That was the time when the princes of Moscow, to frighten their visitors, would hide mechanical lions under their thrones, whose duty was to growl at the right moment and in the right place during the conversation" (*TBD*, 50). The moving force of history is a deception, a make-believe, a simulacrum. The lions of the Russian rulers are mechanical, although they are capable of invoking fear in the audience. Chelyustnikov's beard, cloak, and censer are false, but they still persuade Herriot that there is no religious persecution in the Soviet Union. Every historical event is a repetition of a previous historical event under a new ideological mask that is taken as the sign of the Real in history. "The brutality of the believers in the tyranny of one god was not less barbaric than pagan brutality, and the fanaticism of the believers in the tyranny of one god was still more fierce and efficient" (*TBD*, 37). The shift from pagan polytheism to Christian monotheism is followed by "fierce and efficient" fanaticism, which only increases after Christianity is overturned by the Communist ideology. The new believers are even more fanatical than the old ones. Chelyustnikov's description of the scene in Saint Sophia has a parodic touch that reveals the timelessness of the deception that motivates history. The false priest observes the congregation in the house of God and recognizes all the local Party members. "Next to Comrade Alya, who brought us tea that morning in Comrade Pyasnikov's office, sat the editorial staff and the secretaries of the Provincial Committee, while some of the women, those I couldn't place, were, without doubt the wives of the comrades from Cheka. I have to admit that without exception all played their roles with discipline and dedication"(*TBD*, 46).

To play the role with discipline and dedication means to submit to the will of ideological directives and to show that fanaticism in the new faith is no different from Christian or pagan fanaticism. The only difference is in the misappropriation of the Marxist demand for taking history into one's own hands and deciding its course by active participation, not only by contemplation. Kiš shows how active participation in history is propelled by the same motives as the previous ideologies had—to enslave and rule by promising liberation. Taking history into one's own hands means to repeat the oldest and the cruelest game of deception and violence. Novsky realizes "with horror that this repetition is not accidental, but part of an infernal plan," as in the case of the death of his father at the hands of the Tsar's soldiers. Further, the infernal, circular repetition of the same performance is manifest in the narrator's realization of the identical destinies of Boris Davidovich Novsky in the hands of the Soviet police and Baruch David Neumann in the hands of the Holy Inquisition. "The sudden accidental discovery of this text, the discovery that coincided with the happy completion of the story 'A Tomb for Boris Davidovich,' left me with a feeling of miraculous illumination: the analogy with the story already told is obvious to such a degree that I see the identical motives, dates and names as God's part in creation, *la part de Dieu*, or the devil's, *la part de diable*" (*TBD*, 124).

The narrator discovers that both Boris Davidovich Novsky and Baruch David Neumann display "a consistency of moral beliefs" and that their murder is "the spilling of the sacrificial blood" in the name of the dominant ideological principle (*TBD*, 124). But, apart from an analogy in their historical destiny, the narrator reveals other "facts" that are even more mysterious: "the coincidence in dates of the arrests of Novsky and Neumann (on the same day of the fatal month of December, but with the span of six centuries: 1330–1930)" (*TBD*, 124). The identity between the two apparently unrelated figures is guided by a transcendental principle, but the narrator is not sure whether that principle is divine, "*la part de Dieu*" or infernal, "*la part de diable*." This fact reveals the ambivalent nature of revolutionary history, which is conducted in the name of high moral principles by utilizing diabolical methods to seize and maintain absolute power. The cyclical nature of history is just another sign of the return to the despotic rule of the pagan clan, which now uses the symbols of the red star and the hammer and sickle. The protagonists of *The Tomb for Boris Davidovich* are forced to play their parts "with discipline and dedication" within the circular borderline, which is now reinforced by barbed wire and guarded by tanks and airplanes. Kiš compares the dictatorship of the proletariat with the medieval terror of the Holy Inquisition, because both ideologies (Catholic and Communist) apparently halt the progressive linear movement of history by imposing the despotic circularity of their respective political projects. The destiny of Boris Davidovich marks a return to, and a repetition of, Baruch Neumann's tragic destiny at the hands of the Catholic mob. Both the Christians and the Communists sacrifice individual human beings on the altar of some lofty, abstract principle, which is necessarily an invention projected into the untenable realm of the future. In the Middle Ages, the utopian postulation of a life after death insures the rule of the priesthood and nobility over the material realm, while communism postulates a life to come in the zone of historical evolution and progress.

Kiš brings out the similarity between the medieval and contemporary totalitarian systems of control. The cult of the individual, which characterizes the Modern Age rebellion against the rationally unexamined collective fantasy of the Christian fathers, is destroyed once again, this time by the collective fantasy of the revolutionary brotherhood. Boris Davidovich, like Baruch Neumann, stands up against the collective fantasy in the name of the ethical principles of individualist humanism, derived from a common Jewish source. Kiš alludes to the liberal element of Judaism, which is appropriated and transformed into the apocalyptic teaching about the Second Coming by Christians or transformed into the establishment of a classless society by the Communists. These collective fantasies, propelled by a genuine drive for liberation, are used by those who have the power of the state apparatus behind them to support and justify their authority. Jews, whose isolation and prosecution in Europe insures their marginality, become for Kiš the symbol of individualist rebellion in the face of organized power. Jews are a collective tragic hero who is given many names and faces in *The Tomb for Boris Davidovich.*

the jewish question

In his collection of polemical essays entitled *Čas Anatomije* (*The Anatomy Lesson*), Kiš quotes Freud in order to illustrate his own reasons for introducing the Jewish themes in *The Tomb for Boris Davidovich:* "As a Jew, I was always ready to join the opposition and to renounce every agreement with the compact majority" (*AL,* 51). Kiš claims that the Judaism of his protagonists has the same "form of a latent rebellion," a way of elaborating his firm opposition to the logic of majority rule" (*AL,* 51). This negativity, cultivated by the oppressors of the religious and ethnic minorities (including the Jews) during centuries of European history, is a chief determinant of the fate of Jewish characters in the book. There is no doubt that the Jewish role in the early Communist movement is crucial: starting with Marx's revolutionary philosophy and ending with Trotsky's theory of permanent revolution, the intellectual opposition of the Jews to the views of the dominant power structure contributes significantly to every movement that has liberation and social transformation at its roots. The spirit of rebellion that refuses to identify with the views of the "compact majority" represents a crucial aid to the task of dismantling any totalitarianism, including the Communist one. It is not surprising that the most prominent totalitarian powers of this century, guided by the ideologies of Nazism and communism, were distinctly anti-Semitic. The anti-Semitism of Stalin, no less important than that of Hitler, surfaces in *The Tomb for Boris Davidovich* as one of the latent motivating forces of Kiš's work. Both Dr. Taube and Boris Davidovich Novsky are purged from the Communist movement for no apparent reason, but in the context of their Jewish origin, it becomes clear that they are eliminated *because* they are Jews.

danilo kiš

The Jewish question is introduced in the first chapter through the relationship of Reb Mendel, a Jewish craftsman, and his apprentice Miksha, the man who murders Hanna Krzyzewska on the orders of his Party boss. Reb Mendel complains to Miksha about the hens that are eaten by a skunk every night. "Look for the thief among the Jews," Miksha replies cynically. He suggests that the Jew is a greedy animal like a skunk and that he, too, stinks. "Reb Mendel understood the force of the insult and for some time didn't mention his Cochin hens" (*TBD*, 5). Miksha's anti-Semitism shows the degree to which the Slavs, not unlike the Germans, construct their own national and racial identity by negating the authentic value of Jewish identity. Jewishness is posited as a sign of moral decay and is projected onto the image of the skunk, a solitary predator who survives by devouring other, helpless creatures, which, like hens, live collectively in a common home. This cultural stereotype is used by Kiš to demonstrate the degree to which nationalist and racist prejudices are still endemic in the supposedly "international" Communist movement.

The theme of moral choice made in favor of the other, which is later developed in the case of Boris Davidovich who overcomes his "egocentric attitude" to save the young hostages Fedukin kills to pressure him into signing a false confession, is introduced here for the first time. Although the skunk continues to cause damage to Reb Mendel, the old man's pride does not allow him to mention his problem to Miksha again until only one hen is left. Miksha knows what is troubling the old craftsman, but refuses to acknowledge it. "He waited for the skunk to destroy what it could destroy, and to prove to Reb Mendel that his Talmudic prattle about the equality of all God's creatures was worthless until justice was achieved on earth by earthly means" (*TBD*, 5). At the very beginning of his work, Kiš introduces the struggle of the two opposing moral standards, the one of metaphysical justice represented by the "Talmudic prattle" of the Jews, and the other, based on pragmatism, embodied by Miksha's undigested Marxism. The concept of the achievement of justice "on earth by earthly means" reflects the fearful alliance between the peasant denial of metaphysical justice and the materialist ideology of communism. In Kiš's view, Christianity among the peasants is superficial

and hypocritical, concerned more with immediate material circumstances as they occur in the world. If the skunk has the same right to
life as a hen then a Jew also has the same right to life as a Christian.
Reb Mendel embraces the utopian principle of divine justice: this is a
way of rationalizing his existence through faith in a just God, even
while the persecution of Jews continues around him. The old man
overcomes his indignation and favors the last surviving hen, paradoxically affirming his own material interest and negating his dignity. "Is
it possible that one Cochin hen worth at least five chevronets is equal
to a skunk who robs the poor and stinks far and wide?" Reb asks
Miksha on the ninth day of the silent psychological duel between the
two (*TBD*, 5). His question reveals his own doubt in the equality of
all creatures, implicitly confirming Miksha's prejudice about the inferiority of Jews. "It isn't Reb Mendel. A Cochin hen worth at least five
chevronets can't be compared with a stinking skunk," Miksha replies,
triumphant because the Jew has confirmed his greedy nature (*TBD*,
5). With this silent agreement between the gentile and the Jew, "a
stinking skunk" is sentenced to death.

In this fable-like episode, Kiš reveals the inability of Reb Mendel
to represent his concern for the hen as the utopian principle of God's
ultimate justice because his acts are interpreted by Miksha in accordance with the racial stereotype of the Jew as materially greedy.
Miksha projects his own predatory aggression onto the skunk, con-
tinuing his Jew-skunk identification. That same night he traps the
animal. He is not satisfied with the mere elimination of the skunk
and proceeds to flay it alive. The torture of the animal is a metaphor
of the holocaust, inspired by Kiš's childhood memory from Hungary
about the salutary effect of flaying skunks: "When the skunk is flayed
alive, *az apja bü dös uristenét*, then the *uram*, dear sir, will not dare
show up in the yard for years, no sir, no other skunk, and that's the
way it is. . ." (*AL*, 101). Miksha's help, thus, does not end with the
mere elimination of the skunk; the added cruelty is supposed to repel
other skunks from entering the yard again. "Reb Mendel, I have
released you from skunks once and for all," says the apprentice, rein-
forcing the theme of the final solution (*TBD*, 6). It is as if Miksha
magically cures Reb Mendel of his "skunk nature" by this act of cruelty, enabling him to purge his own Jewishness. The old man senses

this and is unable to endure his brutal insult. "When Reb Mendel finally spoke, his voice sounded hoarse and terrible, like the voice of a prophet: 'Wash the blood off your hands and face. And be damned, Herr Miksat!'" (*TBD*, 6).

Miksha loses his job with Reb Mendel and soon discovers the power of the latter's curse. Nobody in the region of Antonovka is willing to employ him now. "At the mention of Miksha's name, the Jew would rave in Yiddish and Hebrew alternately, beating his breast and pulling his hair as if someone had mentioned a dybbuk" (*TBD*, 7). The Jews know the danger posed by a man who has no respect for the life and suffering of all creatures. Since they are placed somewhere between men and animals on the moral scale of the "compact majority," they know that men like Miksha will gladly exterminate them the moment someone gives the order.

On the other hand, Miksha imagines that the wall of silence the Jews have built around him after his attempt to help Reb Mendel is a sign of ingratitude characteristic of Jewish nature. His anti-Semitism is confirmed and strengthened. "In return, Miksha solemnly swore that one day he would revenge himself for the injury Talmudists had inflicted on him" (*TBD*, 7). Miksha gets his chance to revenge himself when Aimicke, the leader of his Party cell, orders him to kill Hanna Krzyzewska. Although Miksha cannot know that she is Jewish, the evil divinity of chance decides that Hanna is the one to become the first human victim of Miksha's injured pride. "She had freckles on her face (just barely visible now in the twilight of the autumn evening), but they didn't have to be a mark of Cain, those sunspots—maybe a mark of race and the curse, but not a mark of betrayal" (*TBD*, 9). Miksha obeys Aimicke's command and murders Hanna, who is suspected of being a police informer, in the same heartless manner as he had butchered the skunk. "Through the clacking of the train wheels and the muffled thunder of the iron threstle, the girl began, before the death rattle, to speak—in Romanian, in Polish, in Ukrainian, in Yiddish, as if her death were only the consequence of some great and fatal misunderstanding rooted in the Babylonian confusion of languages" (*TBD*, 11).

The narrator returns to the "terrifying moment of Babel," introduced at the beginning of the chapter, to reiterate the consequences of the fracturing of the mythic Ur-code, which causes the "fatal mis-understanding" between the races and nations of the world and results in the eternal persecution of the Jews, the inventors of the myth of a common origin in language. Hanna's death is determined by chance, without any real betrayal on her part. The Communists decide to sacrifice her "since the members of the cell had definite reasons to suspect that someone among them was an informer, he [Aimicke] had to sacrifice one of the members" (*TBD*, 13). History in *The Tomb for Boris Davidovich* appears as a whimsical force whose consequence is always (except in the case of the Irish revolutionary Verschoyle) predictable: it ends up in the sacrifice of the Jews. David Abramovich, Boris Davidovich's father, is humiliated and tortured by the Tsar's soldiers on Christmas Eve because he reads the Talmud while the other soldiers are drinking cognac and celebrating the birth of Christ. The soldiers do not tolerate his religion, and they drag him into the icy river and make him drink alcohol. His son Boris is conceived that night, after David's forced baptism in the Dniepr River. The fact that the title character of the work is born out of love engendered after the forced baptism and torture of his Jewish father points to the tragic determinants of the hero's fate even before his conception. Although the father's origin is never mentioned in the story again, the life of Boris Davidovich evolves under the curse of his Jewish origin.

The sense of family misfortune Kiš describes in his essays on Judaism strongly affected his own destiny. "Judaism in my case, and not only in mine, on the psychological or on the metaphysical level, is a persistent sentiment that Heine called *Familienunglück*, the family misfortune," he writes (*AL*, 50). The apocalyptic sense of doom, confirmed and reinforced by historical facts, creates a specific anxiety that is translated into Kiš's borderline poetics. "In 1944, my father and all our relatives will be taken to Auschwitz, and almost none of them will return."[7] The existential uncertainty caused by the destructive effects of history forces Kiš to seek an identity that is always torn between the language and culture of the home country and the identity constructed through Hebrew, Yiddish, and the wisdom of the Prophets. This is the condition of permanent exile from both cultures, which creates anxiety and *Familienunglück*. "The sentiment of family misfortune is a type of anxiety which, both on the literary and the psychological plane, reinforces the feeling of relativity—which in turn generates irony. And that's all there is to it" (*AL*, 50). The irony renders all absolute cultural values relative and forces one to attempt to survive by the constant deconstruction of one's own identity and culture. This irony, built into the national identity of the small and marginal nations, is caused by an inability to seriously accept the validity of dominant cultural values. Experience of the world is determined by what Russian formalists call "defamiliarization" (*ostranenie*), which is here not just a mere literary device, but an existential and historical fact. This explains Kiš's insistence that his is the "literature of the fact." He is against fantastic literature that invents an alternative, make-believe universe, based on nonsense and imagination. "My mother read novels until she was twenty when, not without regret, she realized that novels are 'invented' and rejected them once and for all. Her aversion to 'mere inventions' is also latent in my writing."[8] Although Kiš's poetics is permeated with the magical comprehension of the connection between all events in the universe, that connection is derived from historical evidence and not from the "mere invention" of literary ornaments. The facts he borrows from historiography are the foundation, the material used for the formation of the plot of his novelistic creations. This orientation toward the paradoxical truth of the literary process is evident in Kiš's writing about Ivo Andrić, another writer who was obsessed with the discovery of novelistic material within history. "The conviction that fantasy is the sister of lie, and therefore dangerous, results in his [Andrić's] poetics which rejects 'the laughable textures of imagination as a shameful deception.'"[9] This poetics starts from the factual material, trying to authenticate the writing practice by developing a *syužet* that resonates with the search of the individual for his identity.[10] This search for a stable identity inevitably fails, however, due to the deceptive and destructive force of the historical process itself. The Jews (and other smaller ethnic groups) are *a priori* placed in the marginal historical position, which defines them as inferior, simultaneously granting them a more acute insight into the relativity of values: they are posited by the dominant ideology, not given as universals.

This insight is developed in the chapter called "Dogs and Books," which represents the poetic matrix for the entire Jewish question in the book. The narrator explores the tragic destiny of Baruch Neumann, Boris Davidovich's double, the historical prototype for the destiny of the borderline nation *par excellence*. Baruch attempts to maintain his individual integrity in spite of the campaign against him led by the Christian majority. Kiš notes that Baruch's story is not his original creation, but a translation from the Inquisition archives. The event takes place during the raid of the fanatical Christian sect of Pastoureaux on the Jews in France. The members of the sect demand that all the Jews either convert to Christianity or die. Baruch attributes their actions to ignorance and a lack of compassion. "I was busy reading and writing," he confesses, "when a great number of these men burst into my chamber, armed with ignorance blunt as a whip, and hatred sharp as a knife" (*TBD*, 113). "The compact majority" does not need to act in a noble manner when relating to Jews—ignorance and hatred are preferable since they reinforce the dominant ideology. Kiš juxtaposes the motivating forces of Christian and Communist anti-Semitism, demonstrating how these two ideologies, which appropriate their fundamental values from Judaism, manage to disguise that fact by cultivating hatred of Jews. "It wasn't my silks that brought blood to their eyes, but the books arranged on my shelves; they shoved the silks under their cloaks, but they threw books on the floor, stamped on them and ripped them to shreds before my eyes" (*TBD*, 113). The Pastoureaux are reflecting the residual pagan fear of the written word, which is not legitimated by the priests of the Christian tribe, as if the physical destruction of the book (the Talmud) will magically extinguish the faith founded on it.

Baruch embodies an ethical standard that does not permit religion to limit itself to the endorsement of an anthropocentric material reality, which has dominated institutional Christianity since Jesus's prophetic performance. This performance allows the Pastoureaux to identify with a central model at the point where ideology (in the form of Christianity) begins to construct and actively transform history within the eschatological horizon of the Second Coming. This apocalyptic horizon demands periodic purges, an unconscious repetition of the first sacrifice of the Jew, that is the Passion of Christ. The compulsive nature of Christianity that purges Christ of his Jewish origin manifests itself in the ominous repetition of the sacrifice. Therefore, the Pastoureaux are allowed to embody the pagan spirit once more and to abandon the moral codes and steal from Baruch, who is always an outsider, a Jew waiting for the Messiah and his own sacrifice. The law is suspended since it does not apply to the Jew who does not accept the original sacrifice as his law. Institutional religion transforms Christ into a vehicle of ignorance and hatred, limiting the horizons of humanism by abolishing and persecuting dissent and difference. Baruch is a symbol of a rebellious minority that, in spite of persecution, continues to challenge the monolithic codes of "the compact majority." "I told them not to rip them [the books] apart, for many books are not dangerous, only one is dangerous; I told them not to tear them apart, for the reading of many books brings wisdom, and the reading of one brings ignorance armed with rage and hatred" (*TBD*, 114).

Baruch's pluralism is the prototype of modern identity, which would soon replace the medieval domination of the religious codes. Judaic ambivalence about the arrival of the Messiah and the end of time allows Baruch to overcome the cognitive limit of the Christian dogma, which is motivated by the realization of teleological narratives in the Christ figure. The monological narrowing of the field of knowledge (both in Christianity and in communism) for the purpose of social control is countered by the plurality of viewpoints contained in Baruch's "many books that bring wisdom." Judaism in Baruch's case is a sign of marginality, which gives him a better perception of the blindness of the majority. "Do not seek other paths besides the one on which everyone walks" is the advice Baruch is given by the Christian clergy (*TBD*, 116). The Pastoureaux believe only in the Gospels, which they advocate with the same fervor as the Communists champion the writings of Marx and Lenin. "Convert, or we'll knock out of your head the wisdom from all the books you've ever read!" is what they shout at Baruch. The wisdom of ambivalence is not tolerated because it is a sign of difference from the established rules of the local society. Therefore, the Jews are, against their own will, placed in the position of exiles and outcasts who are to be converted or exterminated. Baruch takes the position of enlightened ambivalence in deciding his destiny: "Witnessing the blind fury of this mob and seeing them kill before my eyes the Jews who refused to be converted (some out of faith, and others from that pride which can sometimes be perilous), I answered that I would rather be converted than killed, since, in spite of everything, the temporary agony of being is more valuable than the ultimate void of nothingness"(*TBD*, 114).

Baruch negates the basic faith in eschatology, which treats human purpose and destiny in the light of the end of this world and places emphasis on the world to come. He does not deny the "temporary agony of being" because, like the existentialists, he understands death as "the ultimate void of nothingness." He accepts "the temporary agony of being" as a value given by God, in order to prolong his existence and to actively share the suffering of the world. He embraces the borderline condition of a convert, while at the same time attempting to stand outside of all religions, alone before God. During the course of the narrative, Baruch is converted back and forth between Judaism and Christianity until his identity becomes completely stripped of all identifications with religious values. "When we were in the vicinity of the town hall, I told everyone who asked that I was a Jew; but when we passed through the notorious narrow streets and people asked the sergeant if I wasn't perhaps a Jew who refused baptism, he told them as I advised him: that I had been baptized and was a good Christian" (*TBD*, 118).

The switching of identities results from Baruch's withdrawal from the world of God with the sole desire of preserving his bare existence. He can find comfort only within himself, hoping to sustain a space where he can construct his own ethical stand and enact his tragic individuality. This spiritual alienation is another sign of the imminent Modern Age rebellion against the organized repression of perverted Christian ideology. In the end, Baruch rejects Christianity, not simply to defend his Judaism but to uphold the principle of difference. He rejects the uncritical identification with the powerful majority. When questioned by the Inquisitor about his reasons for exposing himself to the "danger of heresy," Baruch replies: "Because I wish to live in peace with myself and not with the world" (*TBD*, 121). God does not figure any longer in this equation, as Baruch attempts to define the space within "myself" that will be removed from the corruption of "the world," a realm that implicitly denies the religious perspective. But he soon wavers and returns to Judaism, then back again to Christianity, until he finally expires under torture in the Inquisitorial chambers. His numerous conversions and identity crises turn him into a horrible caricature of history because he is forced to detach himself from his identifications and becomes a historically borderline subject. Although Judaism is the foundation of Baruch's ethical stand, it quickly erodes under the violent threats of the Christian majority. When he reverts back to Judaism, his ethics has already suffered a defeat, since he now bears the mark of hypocrisy. Every consequent conversion increases the sense of falsehood, further eroding his moral posture, until Baruch's identity is simply subsumed by the Inquisitorial Archives. Kiš states that his poetics is based on the defamiliarizing effect of history on the destiny of Jews. "Judaism in *TBD* has a twofold (literary) meaning: on the one hand, in view of my earlier books, it creates a necessary connection and expands the mythologemes I am involved with, and on the other hand, *Judaism is, like in my earlier books, simply the effect of defamiliarization*" (*AL*, 51; italics in original).

The forces that control European history have created an ironic distance between the inner person and its historical portrait, between the face and the mask. In the case of Jews, who are forced to carry a heavier burden of racial and religious difference and compromise with the dominant codes, the historical identity is borderline by definition. Always at odds with the "compact majority," Jews are forced to accept their borderline status in order to maintain a sense of inner integrity. From the marginal point of view, history always appears as a malignant force, destroying those prepared to defend their difference in spite of the threat of physical annihilation. Kiš sees the destiny of the Jews both as a tragic and an ironic fact of European civilization, which perpetrated numerous genocides on them in order to reinforce the stability of its religious or national myths. Jewish destiny becomes the model for all marginal individuals, regardless of religious or national affiliation, because it shows the relativity of the monolithic programs of ideological control.

Baruch Neumann and Boris Davidovich, historical twins separated by the gap of six centuries, are victimized by the same machinery of total ideological control, whether under the sign of the Catholic cross or of the Communist star. They are both Jews who renounce Judaism in order to become individuals, stripped of all ideology and made to face the organized power of the state from a unique humanist perspective. But their attempts are doomed to failure because Baruch is born before the age of humanism, while Boris is born after its end. These two destinies stand at the borders of an epoch that has seen the rise and the decline of individualism and humanist ethics. In both cases, the individual is annihilated by the torture specialists of the state apparatus, whose task is to decompose and analyze their individuality in order to preserve the ideological purity of the collective illusion.

While Baruch Neumann is the victim of medieval Christian paranoia, Boris Davidovich's destiny opens a perspective on the New Middle Ages inherent in Communist ideology. The initial revolutionary spark that promises liberation of the people is extinguished by Stalin's purges and the destruction of "individualism" in the name of the collective. While Christianity carried out pogroms in the name of the invisible Father and the Son who impersonated him, Soviet communism committed pogroms in the name of a single person, whose name is emblematic of the phantasmatic industrial paradise: Stalin, the Steel One. The man of steel replaces the immaterial God and constructs a monolithic universe according to the principles of science and technology. This universe will not tolerate individualism and difference. Since the Jews are historically defined as the embodiments of difference, they are purged from the revolutionary process. Every deviation threatens the established order, since it implies a change in existing conditions. The Soviet misreading of Marx, whose theory of the Communist revolution presupposes the conscious participation of every individual, leads to the obliteration of individuality in the name of the collectivist dream. The supraindividual becomes the anti-individual, and everyone who thinks, reads, or acts on his own is regarded as a bourgeois individualist who has not given up the so-called "cosmopolitan orientation." The ideological definition of the cosmopolitan, as opposed to the nationalist, carries hidden anti-Semitic overtones, since the pre-Israel Jewish destiny of perpetual exile introduced the new concept of a nation without a land, a nation whose land is the entire world—the very idea of cosmopolitanism.

Kiš's book represents a distillation of the historical experience that has haunted the Communist movement like the shadow of a bad conscience. Embracing the genre of historiographic metafiction, the Yugoslav author probes an emotionally traumatic area of Communist history. Utilizing Borgesian narrative devices, skillfully erasing the border between fact and fiction, Kiš manages to create a work that offers a novelistic critique of Stalinism from an inner, socialist perspective. Unlike Solzhenitsyn, who embraces Christianity and retains the realistic method of narration, Kiš defeats the revolutionary ideology by subverting both the realistic mode of narration and the myth of a stable identity. From the point of view of the victim, he describes the victor as a new man standing on the other side of conventional morality and permitting himself to break all the codes in order to serve a higher, revolutionary ideology. This process of revolutionary destruction establishes a human identity, no longer related to the metaphysical principle that guarantees its meaning and stability. The borderline identity in *The Tomb for Boris Davidovich* depends on the immediate historical circumstance that creates and destroys the protagonists in accordance with the "infernal law of chance." This identity emerges as a construct that is less than human; the human being becomes an effect of the function assigned him by the powers of horror in the universal register of history, a name without a body, an entity offered as a sacrifice to the new gods of totalitarian ideology.

Milan
Kundera:

Lyricism,
Motherhood,
and
Abjection

in

Life

Is

Elsewhere

Life Is Elsewhere is the first novel that the exiled Czech writer Milan Kundera wrote explicitly for the reading public aligned along the Paris–New York axis.[1] In order to bring his novelistic material closer to the reader from a Western historical context, the author displays a radically different sensibility from the one manifest in *The Joke, The Farewell Party, Laughable Loves,* and other works written in Czechoslovakia, which were intended for local consumption. *Life Is Elsewhere* is told in a style that Kundera develops after crossing the border to the West: in this different voice he speaks of the phantasmagoric horror of post-1968 and pre-1989 Czechoslovakian totalitarian reality by absorbing an eclectic blend of popularized versions of existentialism and psychoanalysis. This work contains the rudiments that later become more prominent in Kundera's most popular novels in the West, *The Book of Laughter and Forgetting* and *The Unbearable Lightness of Being*.

The extreme antilyrical tone of this different voice has its origin in the space that opens up for Kundera once he casts off that condition in which he is subsumed by the formative ideological structures of his totalitarian motherland and has crossed over to the realm of the "lightness of being" that dominates the world on the Western side of the border. The separation from his original context resembles a breakdown, an irretrievable loss of placement and being. At the same time, it is a moment in which the ties of abjection are suppressed and disguised, if never fully severed.[2] Kundera's voice is rational, informed, and comical on the surface, because it now springs from "lightness," from a displaced being, endlessly roaming through the gallery of literary figures and historical phantoms that, no longer grounded in the ontolinguistic chora of his mother tongue, are without the existential weight the narrator is searching for.[3]

My reading of *Life Is Elsewhere* emphasizes ways in which Kundera assimilates psychoanalysis in order to turn it inside out, to deny his characters a content of "inner" experience, and to transform the Freudian plot into a motivating force for the narrative voice. By foregrounding his own subjectivity, Kundera shifts the reader's focus away from the characters' psychologies into the external space dominated by existential concerns of death and dissolution. One could say that this is Heidegger's plot voiced by the holy fool: the exploration of the characters' fates is a dialogue between the cynical narrator and his own idealistic youth, situated in the abject universe of Czech historical destiny.

the lyric attitude

The book is divided into seven chapters, five of which are devoted to "the Poet" whose proper name does not appear in the titles of the chapters.[4] The use of this noun instead of the proper name of the main protagonist points to Kundera's desire to immediately move the reader from the particular to the universal plane. This shift becomes even more evident when the reader becomes aware of the juxtaposition of the fate of the central character with the fates of famous poets from literary history: Rimbaud, Lermontov, Shelley. The reader is now assured that this is not just a novel about a poetic dilettante, but a case study of lyricism as a mode of being. Says Kundera: "The lyric attitude is a potential stance of every human being; it is one of the basic categories of human existence. Lyric poetry as a literary genre has existed for ages, because for ages man has been capable of the lyric attitude. The poet is its personification" (Preface to *LIE*, v).

The main vehicle for the expression of the lyric attitude is Jaromil, the only character besides the immortal poets who is named in the novel. Kundera develops his critique of lyricism in the form of a grotesque *Künstlerroman* and investigates the young poet's destiny in a fashion borrowed from the psychoanalytic search for unconscious motivation. The Freudian belief in the decisive influence of early experiences on the formation of character is assimilated and parodied by Kundera at the same time: the analysis of the lyric attitude starts with the experiences of Jaromil's parents even before the poet is born. The novel begins with the question of the poet's origin, posed by the omniscient narrative voice: "Exactly when and where was the poet conceived?" (*LIE*, 3). The answer is not simple and linear; the poet's mother has at least three sentimental and glorified versions to choose from, while the father sticks with the most mundane one, maintaining that the poet was conceived "in a flustered haste, when somebody noisily turned the key in the adjoining apartment" (*LIE*, 3). The mother's choice reveals her attachment to the romanticized cliché: Jaromil was conceived on a certain morning in the pastoral countryside near Prague.

Kundera presents two opposing versions of reality that will guide the poet's relationship to the world around him throughout the novel: the subdued version of the father, which echoes the literary style of naturalism, and the dominant one of the mother, which is a kitschy version of sentimental lyricism. The beginning of the novel could also be read as a reversal of the perspective in *Tristram Shandy*: the mother creates various theories about the conception, while the father seems to be closer to the existential reality that does not allow him to indulge in the mystifications of the past. "Father's world," however, is only a vague presence in this book, a background against which the destructive power of mother's overblown imagination achieves its full extent. For Kundera, the dominant role of the mother is the determining factor in the formation of the lyric attitude. "Lyric poets generally come from homes run by women: the sisters of Esenin and Mayakovski, the aunts of Blok, the Grandmothers of Hölderlin and Lermontov, the nurse of Pushkin and, above all, of course, the mothers—the mothers that loom so large over the fathers. Lady Wilde and Frau Rilke dressed their sons as little girls. Is it a wonder that the boy kept gazing anxiously at the mirrors? *It is time to become a man,* Orten wrote in his diary. The lyric poet spends a lifetime searching for signs of manhood on his face" (*LIE*, 97).

The problem of the practically absent father and the domination of the mother's imaginary demand becomes the most acute feature in the development of Jaromil's character. The poet is never able to fully sever the invisible ties of abjection that prevent him from reaching the actualized sense of selfhood and differentiation from the maternal. This prevents Jaromil's maturation into an autonomous, ethical subject and turns him instead into a pale caricature of Apollo, his mother's ideal of love and beauty.

Repression of the paternal is manifest in the plot of *Life Is Elsewhere*. The mother alienates the father from Jaromil's life because he wanted their future child aborted. She is not able to forgive him for this attempted betrayal until Jaromil's father is arrested by the Gestapo and killed in a concentration camp. At that point, the mother's imaginary mechanisms are reactivated: the image of her husband is transformed from that of an irresponsible pleasure seeker into that of a war hero. His photograph is framed and put on the wall above her bed: the pleasure she derives from mourning her dead husband is much more intense than the pleasure she was able to experience when he was alive.[5] Distortion is the mother's central psychological mechanism: she is able to transform reality into imaginary phantasms at will. This parodic pleasure principle is responsible for the entire destiny of her son: during her pregnancy, the mother invents Jaromil's fictional father.

In the bedroom was the small table topped by a heavy disk of gray marble on which stood a figurine of a nude male; in his left hand the figure was holding a lyre, propped against his hip. . . . According to the inscription chiseled into the base, the figure with the lyre represented the Greek god Apollo. . . . As she gazed into his comely face she conceived the wish that the child growing in her abdomen would resemble this graceful rival of her husband's. She hoped for a resemblance so strong that she could look at her child and imagine this Greek youth to be his real father. She begged the god to use his powers and change the past, to change the story of her son's conception, to repaint it as the great Titian once painted a masterpiece over a bungler's ruined canvas. (*LIE*, 7)

Kundera's treatment of Apollo and of his reproduction in the guise of newly born Jaromil is one of the central focuses of the novel. The mother's imagination is so powerful that it can counter the reality posed by the narrative voice and change events according to the demands of her present psychological situation. She even goes so far as to beg Apollo to alter the past and the story of her son's conception, thereby manifesting Kundera's belief that the ideals of motherhood are synonymous with those of the totalitarian state, which rewrites its own history.

The figurine of Apollo that supports Mother's imagination is a part of the kitschy bourgeois setting in which the poet's parents live. Kundera is able to turn the trivial into the metaphysical in a split second and to invoke the reality that hides behind appearances. The father supplies a parodic balance: he often throws his smelly socks on top of Apollo to show his symbolic rebellion against the snobbish values of his wife. The Greek god of form and beauty functions as an imaginary construct in the mind of the middle-class mother, who "had learned to love the sentimental gravity of music and books" (*LIE*, 8). Her escapist daydreaming at times reaches the level of pathological fixation. "When she undressed before the mirror, she tried to examine herself through his [Apollo's] eyes: sometimes she seemed enchanting, at other times uninteresting. She surrendered her body to the judgement of someone else's eyes—and that was a source of anxious uncertainty" (*LIE*, 9).

Thus, the figurine of Apollo serves as a field for the mother's projections. His imagined gaze elicits her self-perceptions and, as she enters that field, her identity suffers a split (*Spaltung*): on the one side is the gaze of her own husband (the abject part of her personality); on the other, the gaze of the marble figurine of Apollo (her own "lyric" self). She is completely aware of how "with her milk there flowed into her little son her deepest thoughts, concepts and dreams" (*LIE*, 10). This split is transferred to Jaromil: later in the book, it is manifested as his strong fascination with love and beauty (an attempt to turn abjection into its opposite) and in a self-destructive attitude. This self-destructiveness is his principal legacy from his sustained symbiotic union with the mother. Since her power of imagination is stronger than her ability to cope with reality, Jaromil's identity is dominated by that imaginary demand. As the pregnancy progresses, there is a change in the direction of the gaze that forms her identity. During the course of poet's fetal existence, his mother observes this. ". . . it [the mother's body] ceased to be a mere object of someone else's eyes, and became a living body devoted to someone who as yet had no eyes. Its outer surface lost its importance; it was touching another body along an interior, invisible surface. The eyes of the outer world could thus grasp only its unimportant external envelope. The engineer's [father's] judgement no longer had any significance, for it could in no way influence the body's great destiny" (*LIE*, 10).

The conflict that occurs as a result of the struggle between the gazes of the real and the imaginary father is resolved with the movement of the gaze toward her interior, "to someone who as yet has no eyes," to the formless fetus whose destiny depends entirely on her desire. The gaze that elicits that desire does not belong to the real father, but to the god whom the poet's mother wishes to be the real father. So, the mother gazes at her own interior through the eyes of Apollo, identifying the gaze of that someone "who as yet has no eyes" with the gaze of Apollo. The process of preparing the ground for the poet's birth is directed away from identification with his real father, since "the Poet" is not being born to follow the Freudian model of initiation into manhood, but to assume the role that his frustrated mother and Greek mythology have already created for him.[6] As soon as the poet is born, the mother experiences a sense of unity and symbiosis that she will not renounce until the end of the poet's tragicomical life. "It was a *paradisiac* state: the body was allowed to be a body, and had no need to cover itself with a figleaf; mother and son were submerged in infinite tranquility; they lived together like Adam and Eve before they had tasted of the fruit of knowledge; they lived in their bodies beyond good and evil" (*LIE*, 11).

Kundera's critique of the maternal principle assumes the dimension of a mythic generalization in spite of his rampant opposition to every form of totalizing discourse. This ambivalent mechanism seems to underlie all of his poetics: deny unto others that which you allow yourself. The author appropriates the controlling power of the maternal position, while at the same time denying real-life motherhood. He does so by utilizing an overwhelming narrative voice that treats characters as puppets whose strings are being pulled by the omnipotent author. The "long leash" that the mother ties around Jaromil's neck is Kundera's creation. It is used to subject his fictional characters to the tyranny of Kundera's existential meditations. The only difference is the author's position: he has lost his claim to paradise and proceeds to meditate on the world as a being doomed to eternal fall.

maman's mirrors

A complete separation never takes place during the poet's life because he always remains attached to the imaginary construct of his mother's body and her desire, symbolized by the gaze of Apollo. His mother wishes him to remain an ephebus, a youth who never masters the separation from infantile bliss. Kundera addresses his protagonist directly: "Every time you leave the house you will carry with you a look of reproach, calling you back! You will walk the world like a dog on a long leash! Even when you are far away you will still feel the collar around your neck! And even when you are with women, even when you are lying in bed with them, a long leash will be attached to your neck and somewhere far, far away Maman will hold its end in her hands, feeling from its vibrations the shameful movements of your body!" (*LIE*, 121).

Every time Jaromil tries to place a woman in his life, the invisible leash of abjection reminds him that his mother demands that he remain an identity constructed by her imaginary demands.[7] Mother's desire is responsible for Jaromil's love of poetry: by decorating Jaromil's room with panels inscribed with his words, she is the first one to show the importance of the written sign. As long as her son remains in the world of poetry, she is in control of his love and destiny. The deeper he descends into the illusion of words, the greater is his sense of boundless joy derived from an oceanic merger with the maternal. "But when out of the corner of his eye he glimpsed his own words spread across the room, solid, more permanent, bigger than himself, he was enraptured; it seemed to him that he was surrounded by his own self, that there was so much of him—he filled a room, he filled a whole house" (*LIE*, 19).

The discovery of his own words is tantamount to the discovery of a second existence for Jaromil. The self reflected in his own words on the wall of the room is much more pleasing than reality since it gives him a sense of his greatness. But this symbolization is never in the service of the Real—it is dominated by the imaginary expansion of Jaromil's self that makes him abominable both to his peers and to adults. Later, during his adolescent years, when he confronts the world of women that he is not able to master, Jaromil panics on seeing the reflection of his face in the mirror. This is the moment in which he realizes that his sexual identity is endangered. The self reflected in the visual field is telling him how his face is effeminate and silly, how the influence of his mother is so present in it that he cannot assume the appearance of a grown-up male. His psyche lacks the Oedipal identification with the father, the mark of symbolic castration. But, instead of acting within the real context, he constantly rediscovers the talking mirror of his poetry:

> The hours spent in front of the mirror always plunged him to the very bottom of despair. Fortunately, however, there was another mirror which raised him to the stars. That heavenly mirror was his poetry; he thirsted for the verse he had not yet written and for that already created, he recollected his poems with the pleasure men get from remembering beautiful women; he was not only their author, but their theoretician and historian; he wrote essays about his poetry, he classified his works into individual

stages, he designated these epochs with names, so that in the course of two or three years he learned to regard his poetry as a process of development worthy of a literary historian's loving attention. (*LIE*, 98)

Apollo and Narcissus walk hand in hand: Jaromil's poetry is invested with his own libidinal love; he thrives only in the universe of his highly eroticized word.[8] In order to substitute for the absence of the father, Jaromil engages in a game of multiple mirrors: not only does he write the poems, he also interprets and classifies them and reflects on the reflection. The mechanism is the one already observed in his mother: since reality is not negotiable, the imaginary control of the world is attempted through the use of language. Kundera's critique of sentimentalism is manifested again. Since reality is the source of constant frustration, the poet flees into the world of imagination to rediscover his enlarged self. The acute failure of each of his attempts to deal with the Real originates in the pathological attachment to his mother. The transference of psychological mechanisms between mother and son shows that Jaromil has incorporated his mother's imaginary phantasms, since he lacks the paternal instance. His control of language always serves the narcissistic purpose and never evolves into an art devoted to the other. The phantom of Apollo, of good classical form, hovers over Jaromil through his mother's gaze. In Kundera's universe, this is not sufficient for true artistic achievement. The only instance that can bring about a return to the Real is Jaromil's father, who, at this moment in the novel, is in the concentration camp. The narrator's patrophilic credo is apparent here: the true artist needs a father.

But there are moments of hope; as the father's replacement, Kundera introduces an artist whom the mother meets during one of her vacations with Jaromil. At first, the artist seems like an ideal father substitute: he acts as an authority and, at the same time, being an artist, gratifies the gaze of Apollo. The mother has an affair with the artist, but gives up when the mirror shows that her body is ugly. Her own abjection tells her that she cannot live up to the ideal that the artist has created out of her, mainly because her body has been deformed by pregnancy. Jaromil, who takes drawing classes from the artist, becomes the cause of his mother's inability to have a lover.

milan kundera

Many years later, at the end of his unsuccessful love affair with a college student, the adolescent poet finds himself at a party in the artist's studio. The Nazi occupation is over and the new socialist realist doctrine has invaded the realm of "pure" art. It is the period of post-revolutionary persecution of surrealism and all "bourgeois" art. The apartment of the artist is one of the last bastions of resistance and of European avant-gardism. Everyone there is engaged in a lively intellectual discussion, but Jaromil is silent and melancholic. The crowd in the artist's studio is obviously aware of his poetry and he slowly becomes the center of attention. "And because he realized that he was again the target of attention, he became painfully aware of his face and with mounting apprehension felt that its expression was his mother's smile! . . . He felt that his mother was attached to his head, that she had spun herself around him like a cocoon enveloping a larva, depriving him of the right to his own likeness. . . . This feeling was so painful that Jaromil gathered all his strength to shake off his mother's face, to break loose. He tried to enter the discussion" (*LIE*, 147).

While he is silent, Jaromil is under the spell of his mother's reflection—he carries her smile on his lips. The image is truly psychotic. The mother is a cocoon around him that does not let him develop his own identity. There is only one way of breaking loose from the image of puerile helplessness: he has to start talking, using the word in a different way, as a medium that would invoke the identity of his absent father. Jaromil knows that if he wants to participate in the discussion, the right thing to do is to mention Breton or Dali. But a strange thing occurs: without willing it, he starts attacking the avant-garde as an outmoded movement of degenerate bourgeois artists. He praises the socialist revolution as the only event that answers to Rimbaud's demand for absolute modernity. The voice of the unconscious suddenly breaks loose and starts speaking in terms of the mass ideology of totalitarianism—he affirms the ideals of socialist realism imitating the artist's intonation. "It was actually a strange debate of the artist with himself, the artist-man with the artist child, the artist with his rebellious shadow. Jaromil realized it and felt even more humiliated; and so he expressed himself more and more sharply, in order to revenge himself on his mentor for the gestures and the voice that made him a captive" (*LIE*, 149).

Jaromil is caught between the Scylla of his mother's face and the Charybdis of the artist's voice, desperately trying to ground his own subjectivity. But he ends up in a hall of parallel mirrors: his subjectivity is never real. Jaromil's sexual identity cannot reach the ideal of manhood that he aspires to. The young poet cannot find his own voice because the paternal principle is removed from the foreground by the dominant mother. The artist is not a good model for Jaromil, since the world of surrealism that he represents has been defeated by the new socialist art. At this moment Jaromil's manhood becomes the central problem: "But there was something even more precious than his poems, something that he had never possessed and for which he had been yearning with all his heart: his manhood. He knew that it could be won only through courageous action; and if that courage meant that he was to be totally alone, that he was to renounce his girl, his artist friend, even his poems—so be it; he decided to dare" (*LIE*, 150).

Jaromil stops writing poetry and starts studying political science. "There is time when every poet tears himself away from his mother and starts running" (*LIE*, 161). Jaromil's bid for freedom from the invisible leash ends in his activities at the university, which are characterized by the rebellion against the old world of bourgeois values. He continues to check his face for signs of manhood, but the mirror is not the place to look for it. "He is always surrounded by the wall of mirrors, and he cannot see beyond. For maturity is indivisible; it is either complete or it does not exist at all" (*LIE*, 164). Jaromil realizes that he will never be "a real man" unless he does something about his sexual life. His idea of seduction is predatory: during one of the socialist youth parades, he daydreams about the abduction of the salesgirl from the corner store. "He thinks of the girl imprisoned in the cashier's cage and a terrible sadness comes over him; he dreams of a daring feat: he breaks the store window with a hammer, pushes terrified shoppers aside, opens the cashier's cage and carries off the liberated brunette, to the amazed stares of onlookers" (*LIE*, 177).

Kundera's ironic attitude toward the socialist revolution is manifested in Jaromil's sexual fantasy. Although the poet comes from a solid bourgeois family, socialist realist imagery provides him with a phallus substitute: the hammer, a sign of working-class power, becomes the tool for getting the girl in his daydream. A few days later, Jaromil really enters the store and finds out from a redheaded salesgirl that the brunette he likes is not working there anymore. However, the substitution of identities is smooth and easy in the kingdom of poetic metaphor: the redhead invites him to her apartment, and, before he knows it, Jaromil is initiated into manhood. The metaphorical substitution itself, then, is revealed as the mechanism of love.

Jaromil always takes illusions for reality. After lovemaking with the redhead, new hopes are awakened in him. He starts writing poetry again. His mother is delighted with the change, although she does not know that this has been caused by another woman in Jaromil's life. "It seemed to her that Apollo's lyre was again victorious over her husband's military uniform, and she quietly rejoiced" (*LIE,* 186). When the poet starts demanding a room of his own where he can bring the redhead, the mother is suddenly repelled by the idea of her son's sexuality. Instead of seeing this development as a chance for her own greater freedom, "her disgust over her son's physicality is stronger than the longing of her own body for physical gratification: this insight terrified her" (*LIE,* 190). The bond between the poet and his mother is reinforced since she knows the only way to his heart, the way of lyricism. From the depths of abjection, the mother starts praising him as a poet, and Jaromil soon represses his demand for autonomy. "Jaromil was drinking in his mother's words, overjoyed. It was true. The angel of his childhood understood him better than anybody else! How depressed he had been because he had stopped writing!" (*LIE,* 191).

Jaromil's poetics changes. Instead of intimate, free verse meditations, he starts writing rhymed odes to the proletariat. His poetry shifts from the topics of love, death, and old age to didactic verse about Party men fighting injustice and liberated socialist women riding tractors. He wants to write poetry that will be understood by everyone, but especially by his redheaded girlfriend. For a while it seems that this revolutionary ardor is helping him become an autonomous subject, "a real man." He reconciles the worlds of poetry and reality by writing in a socialist realist manner and is admired by both his mother and his lover. But this is not satisfying to Jaromil, since what he really desires is the impossible: the approval of the absent paternal ideal.

At the same time he invents Xavier, his fictional alter ego. "Xavier lived completely differently from other people; his life was a dream. He slept, and had a dream, and in that dream he fell asleep and had another dream, and from that dream he awoke to find himself in a previous dream. And so he passed from one dream to another and lived several different lives simultaneously" (*LIE*, 197).

Xavier is a creature from the world of dreams, which is more real than reality itself. He is able to experience the full presence of being because he is aware of the illusory nature of reality. He embodies Heidegger's ideal of constant confrontation with the possibility of death, which is the source of true being-in-the-world. Jaromil longs for this ideal, without realizing that behind Xavier's courage is the acceptance of mortality. During his relationship with the redhead, the fictional Xavier is incorporated into a private game. She starts calling the poet by variations of the name, Xavy or Xavik. The mirror of love proves to be the most powerful of all: Jaromil uses the redhead to recapture the pleasure of immersion in his own fantasy world, to pretend that he is like Xavier, just passing from one dream to the other. Kundera reminds the reader that boundless imagination is dangerous. The demand Jaromil's imagination makes on the redhead merges with his mother's demand on himself: he wants to possess the redhead absolutely, together with her past and her future. His jealousy is aroused even when he thinks about some anonymous doctor's hand touching her body. This is the ideology of lyricism: everything is frozen in the monolithic purity of the world before the Fall. "That's why young people are such passionate monists, emissaries of the absolute; that's why the poet weaves his private world of verse" (*LIE*, 220).

Jaromil is really upset when the redhead announces that her brother is coming to visit from the country. He cannot stand the idea of another man sharing the room with his beloved. His insane jealousy reaches a climax when the redhead is late for their date and, as an excuse, invents a story about a meeting with the same brother who is supposed to visit her. She makes up a dramatic account of her brother's plans to emigrate from Czechoslovakia. Of course, Jaromil is being duped: the redhead is actually meeting with her middle-aged lover, a fact the reader learns later in the book. The moment of Jaromil's moral degradation is linked with the final apotheosis of his manhood. Enraged, he writes a letter to the police, denouncing the redhead and her invented brother: "And so he put down his pen and gave himself over to daydreams; he dreamt of a mysterious threshold which a youth must cross in order to become a man; he knew the name of that threshold: its name was not love, it was duty. . . . After all, he wasn't writing about duty in the old sense of the word, imposed by external authority, but duty which man creates for himself, which he chooses freely, a duty which is voluntary and represents human daring and dignity" (*LIE*, 263).

This is a moment of identification with the state and the police, which substitute for the paternal instance missing in Jaromil. His beloved is imprisoned as a result of this dutiful behavior, but he finds a way to rationalize his decision to denounce her to the police, claiming to himself that he has done it out of love, out of his earnest desire for her to become a good citizen. Do we buy this? Can anybody be so foolish? Kundera's answer is yes; the intoxication of the poet knows no boundaries and is, thus, similar to maternal love. And while his lover is in prison, Jaromil's jealousy dissipates. "Why should Jaromil be jealous? The redheaded girl now belonged to him more than ever: her fate was his creation; it was his eye watching her as she urinated into the pail; it was his hand touching her when a guard treated her roughly; she was his victim, his creation; she was his, his, totally his own!" (*LIE*, 266).

Jaromil's identification with the state and the police is the final stage of his participation in the structure of abject power. Now that the girl is safely locked away in the state prison, the hands that may touch her body are part of the same organism as his own hands. He becomes "a real man" as he merges with the corrupt body of the state and her organs of power. Jaromil's search for sexual identity and for his absent father produces its opposite: a further merger with the maternal principle that dominates the abjection of the totalitarian state. Jaromil starts reading his poetry to Prague policemen and meets a woman who uses Police Club funds to direct a movie about the poet's life. When the movie is released, the beautiful director organizes a party. This is Jaromil's last trial and failure, a moment when the lyrical world yields to the power of death. Unwary of the danger, he is ready to make the final leap demanded by the romantic spirit. Jaromil is invited and plans to conquer the director, as a "real man." "And now the moment had come to eliminate the conflict between dream and reality, between poetry and life, between action and thought. To end the split between Xavier and Jaromil both had to merge into a single being. The man of fantasy must become the man of action, the adventure of dreams the adventure of life" (*LIE*, 291).

In the typical Kunderian inversion of a character's intention and destiny, the scene of love is transformed into a scene of death. At the party, the filmgirl introduces him to several people, but Jaromil wants to talk only to her. The director leads him into her room, which is full of people. There, Jaromil is confronted with a young man who calls his poetry "disgusting shit." This insult shakes the foundations of Jaromil's being: the domain of highest idealism is revealed as a sign of lowest abjection. He is ready to challenge his opponent physically and demonstrate his manhood. But he is weaker: after an altercation, Jaromil is thrown out onto the freezing balcony, wearing only a shirt. His pride does not allow him to return and be seen by the crowd that has witnessed his humiliation. He gets pneumonia and dies a few days later.

the ideology of abjection

Kundera's vision of totalitarian reality reverses the usual Western perspective—the state as the realm of the Father and his Law is *not* possible under totalitarian systems. The official atheism has debunked God the Father as the guiding principle and model of human conduct and morality. But can it be that the ideology of the totalitarian state is founded on the appropriation of the destructive maternal principle? Are mothers responsible for the paranoid system of values that does not tolerate ideological difference?

The connection between the oppressive maternal principle that does not permit the separation of the infant and the new Communist state that does not tolerate the opposition and autonomy of its subjects looms in the depths of Kundera's own abjection. In his case, the ideology of abjection is the abjection of ideology. Jaromil's mother is a manifestation of an ideological force that demands absolute conformity with its demands. For those who glorify her, there is a world of cheap sentimentality; for those who oppose her, there is a world of internal exile.[9] This is a sign of Mother Russia, an ambivalent sign of *otherness* that horrifies Kundera: "I want simply to make this point once more: on the eastern border of the West—more than anywhere else—Russia is seen not just as one more European power but as a singular civilization, an *other* civilization."[10]

Note the use of the passive mood: "Russia is seen . . ." Who sees her? This is the moment when Kundera becomes Jaromil—he speaks in the name of someone else, in the name of the oppressed Czech people, in order to sever the invisible leash that the Dark She has tied around his neck. The abjection caused by his historical fate breaks through the transparent surface of his narrative and shows the shadow of the Dark She: yes, there is an instance of this abject politics, a mother figure who does not allow her helpless children to speak out in their own voice, whether that voice be Czech or Bulgarian.[11]

The convergence of politics and psychology on a single plane of human destiny is Kundera's main interest. Jaromil's struggle for manhood and maturity takes place under the same sign as the struggle of the small Czechoslovakian state to deny and reject the power of Russia and her maternal "Slavic soul." This commonplace designation of the proto-Slavic source, which originates in the pagan myth of the "Damp Mother Earth," represents something that Kundera wants to eliminate from his universe, to relegate to beyond the eastern border of the West. "I, too, know of nothing more ridiculous than this cult of obscure depths, this noisy and empty sentimentality of the 'Slavic soul' that is attributed to me from time to time."[12]

This statement is symptomatic of abjection: an intellectual denial of the Slavic element tied to the "cult of obscure depths," the internal police, thinly disguised in "the noisy and empty sentimentality" that is a prominent characteristic of nearly all Kundera's female characters.[13] The Czech language is Slavic, and it embodies the residues and resonances of that proto-Slavic culture that Kundera wishes to repress or define as *otherness*. How does he explain the untranslatability of *Litost* into any of the Western cultural codes? Is there not something specific about Slavic cultures? The problem is that Kundera associates the "Slavic soul" with the ideological domination of Mother Russia. Only from the other side of the border, in the relative security of his enlightened Westernness, can he articulate the abjection that boils under the surface of his smart prose and his effortless elegance.

Kundera refuses to participate in any poetic activity that is born out of an *affirmation of the ideal*. His parody exposes all lyrical values as projections of the abject union of the poetic subject with the pseudo-matriarchal ideology of communism or of any other form of revolutionary idealism. His negative stance toward the Apollonian is directed against every form of idolatry and marks the withdrawal of the subject from the stage of ideology and its abjections.

For Kundera, life is on the side of the hedonistic middle-aged man with whom the redhead has sex while she lies to Jaromil and claims that she is meeting with her brother. The reader recognizes the principle Kundera sees as lacking in ideology: the middle-aged man represents values of the low, the simple, and the mundane, and he belongs to common-sense culture, which rejects all ideological demands as transparent lies. However, the middle-aged man does not persist in his negative attitude throughout the novel, because he affirms solitary hedonism, the *ideology of the body*. Have a bite of good food, read something interesting, and make love to a girl or two. He is also the only character in the book capable of true compassion and understanding: when the redhead is released from the prison, he selflessly takes care of her.

Kundera the cynic overcomes negativity and identifies with the values that are embodied by the bachelor's belly. In the process, he betrays a sympathy for the man who shuns high and lofty ideals of the masses while indulging in existentialism without responsibility. "He [the middle-aged man] concentrated entirely on himself, on his responsibility-free amusements and his books" (*LIE*, 280). This concentration on oneself, possible after identification with the father, is a value that Kundera opposes to the pseudo-matriarchal universe of totalitarianism. Without abjection, there is nothing to dread—identity can be formulated as a surface without weight and resistance, subsumed by media or a lifestyle. The middle-aged man's way of confronting the falsity and abjection of mass phantasms is to intentionally withdraw into alienation imposed by the official ideology. Kundera glorifies this form of alienation, since it accepts the weight of abjection, which has long ago been exterminated, sublimated, or marginalized in the West, where being is seen as possessing "the unbearable lightness." Opposing and resisting the lyrical merger, the middle-aged man cultivates his autonomy in forgetfulness, accepting existential dread with irony that heals. This is the position that promises survival in spite of the destructive totality that tricks and kills Jaromil and the entire generation of lyrical souls who are unable to break the abject ties with the universe of pseudo-matriarchal totality.

The
Rise
of
the
Nation:

From
the
Margin
to
the
Center

Many unexpected events continue to undo the political, social, and cultural fabric of "the lands-in-between." The general trend of liberalization will certainly bring many changes in the relationship between the political ideology and cultural identity in the region, as a result of the inevitable separation of the Central and Eastern European "infants" from the body of the "abjectly maternal" Soviet Union, which has been dissolved and transformed back into "Mother Russia." Political transformation may be beneficial for both sides if it results in a different set of cultural practices. But the rise of nationalism threatens to substitute one form of totalitarian control with another, this time founded on the much more dangerous myths of common blood and soil. Nationalist exaltations have already caused the breakup of Yugoslavia and continue to drag the South Slavs deeper into the war between the Catholic Croats and Orthodox Serbs. Lotman's dual model is confirmed here: after Titoism failed as a dominant ideology, it was replaced by the older cultural formation of Christianity, divided into its Western and Eastern articulations. Instead of progressing into a new zone of liberal democracy, culture is taken over by war and regression to the state of affairs that existed there before 1941 and even before 1914. Individual nations re-invent their pasts and return to "fundamental" values of religion as a key factor in the formation of cultural identity. The totality known as "communism" is rapidly vanishing as a political model, to be replaced by the smaller, nationalist totalities. The literary forces are now pushed into the background or replaced with writers who glorify the past of the nation in question.

Borderline writing, with its obsessive negation of institutionally imposed limits, paradoxically, finds itself in a vacuum created by the sudden absence of totalitarian control. The plurality demanded by the masses is generally focused on material wealth and positive economic growth. Writing has lost some of its aura of martyrdom as it emerges from underground and achieves its long-awaited autonomy from politics. It is certain, however, that nationalism, as an emergent institutional logic, is restructuring itself under a different sign and is inhabiting the vacuum left by the demise of the one-party control. The restoration of national ideals is bound with popular culture, which worships blood, soil, and the glorious past of ancestors, evoking the formulas that once more affirm mass belief at the expense of the individual and often negative vision of the marginal writer.

The comparative study of Slavic cultures in the period between the revolution of 1917 and the abolition of totalitarianism in 1989 is central to any analysis of regimes and codes that inform the Slavic variety of marginal culture and literature. As they explore the phenomena rooted in the negative, obverse side of dominant cultural practice, these borderline texts simultaneously aspire to embody the essence of artistic freedom—as Bulgakov's Master does—and to overcome the mere technological mastery of literary genres. Accepted literary and cultural codes are mutilated because they pretend to represent the totality, a magical version of reality enforced by both the national and Party ideology. Franz Kafka expressed this anarchic tendency of all the great marginals when he wrote about the inherent tendency to "tear madly at the bonds" imposed by the threatening edifices of the state and its bureaucratic apparatus. "Human nature, essentially changeable, unstable as the dust, can endure no restraint; if it binds itself it soon begins to tear madly at its bonds, until it rends everything asunder, the wall, the bonds and its very self."[1]

While searching for literary forms that would further problematize ideology and identity, the marginal writer exposes layers of culture that are threatened with erasure by every form of monocultural totalitarianism, often risking his own destruction. From Bulgakov's novelistic deconstruction of vulgar materialism and Gombrowicz's refusal of ideological masks in the 1930s to Kiš's poetics of historical horrors and Kundera's analysis of abjection in the 1970s, we have seen how this particular type of fiction examines institutional power from the position of an individuality that has been exploited, scorned, persecuted, and exiled by the instruments of ideological control. This type of artistic practice resists definitions and illusions of political progress, rejecting the narcissistic posturing and naiveté of the avant-garde. It is motivated by *thought*, not by the desire to break away from verisimilitude or to adequately represent the totality of artistic worldview. Independent thought, regarded as a deviation in the majority of (both Communist and nationalist) political systems, is a foundation for this type of writing practice, which has invested heavily in a new brand of critical rationalism. Questioning the scientism inherent in modernist neophilias, the thought finds its material in the ironic, deconstructive dismantling of the ideological universe that depends on the binary opposition. Julia Kristeva, formulating the problem of dissidence, attempts to find a mode of thought that resists technology and its binary structures, avoiding the idealist trap of the Hegelian master/slave dialectic and affirming difference in the face of all forms of identity: "For true dissidence today is perhaps simply what it has always been: *thought*. Now that Reason has become absorbed by technology, thought is tenable only as an 'analytic position' that affirms dissolution and works through differences. It is an analytic position in the face of conceptual, subjective, sexual and linguistic identity."[2]

Kristeva's position is symptomatic of an exiled subjectivity, a subjectivity that is forced to use thought as a weapon in the struggle against the institutions and their supposed rationality that yields the irrational results of global politics. By overcoming the conceptual limitations of the externally imposed identity, "a new type of intellectual" creates works that always question the motivation of both sides of the master/slave dialectic in order to overturn the very conditions for the functioning of the law of binary opposition. "There is no law but the law of death. To acknowledge this may help us to cause fewer deaths with the law."[3] This fatalistic assessment, which equates *logos* and *thanatos*, grounded in Freud's *Totem and Taboo,* opens a dimension outside the infinite play of oppositions that causes death and flirts with the ultimate apocalypse. Thought finds itself outside institutional rationality while desiring the literary atopia, a position closer to the Real, because it denies the phantasmatic ordering of "reality." Kundera agrees: "To base a novel on a sustained meditation goes against the spirit of the twentieth century, which no longer likes to think at all."[4] By constructing identities that claim to have experienced the other side of their identity, these writers seek to think through the obverse of language: depression, madness, cruelty, and horror.

Bulgakov's utopian solution at the end of *The Master and Margarita* prefigures Kristeva's anarchistic call for the position outside of all identities. The Master, who ends up inhabiting the world of his own fictional creation, is a parodic precursor of the new intellectual, whose borderline status is not only a necessity, but also an ethical imperative. Bulgakov affirms the romantic posture through double negation—he invents a fictional world to negate reality and then parodies that world and thus again negates it—and is exulted by the "truth" of his own fiction about the conflict between the individual and the institution. The Master's obsession with Pilate, rather than with Christ, reflects Bulgakov's attempt to penetrate into the mythical origins of the Christian superego, the power constituting literary truth through denial of institutional formations. The

Christian subtext of the novel is symbolic of the Master's tragic transcendence and Bulgakov's longing for the feminine space represented by Margarita, a dimension destroyed by the pseudo-matriarchy of the Bolsheviks.

Gombrowicz, a figure torn between social conformism and the phallic desire to explode every convention, is perhaps the most extreme example of the borderline prosaist. Oscillating between narcissism and disavowal, he discharges a torrent of language that exposes the beliefs and the ideologies responsible for European catastrophes and holocausts. *Ferdydurke* is a precious document of eternal adolescence, a determined rejection of the destructive and hypocritical adult world that is abandoned in the name of a simulated inadequacy and immaturity. Although politically and sexually marginalized, Gombrowicz finds a way of avoiding sublimation in writing, turning himself against every stable identity that he might possibly inhabit. What remains is a parody of "modern living" and a critique of an identity whose idealized surfaces cover an imperfect, all-too-human core.

Kiš's destiny manifests the historical origins of the poetics of borderline fiction. Born in Hungary to a Jewish father and a Montenegrin mother, moved to Yugoslavia to escape the anti-Semitic laws in Hungary, returned to Hungary after the 1942 Novi Sad massacre, he was baptized into the Serbian Orthodox Church, then forced to attend the Hungarian Catholic Sunday School. Historical and political traumas affect Kiš before he is even ten years old, creating the conditions for a particularly uncanny vision of the historical process. Concentrating on the Comintern, Kiš uses historiographic material as a foundation for the prosaic rethinking of individual destiny. The poetics of horror that permeates *The Tomb for Boris Davidovich* is engendered by the powers of history that are represented as random, ruthless, and blind. The totalitarian ideology is just another mask, behind which power may stalk its victims, who are naive enough to believe in the reality of that mask.

Kundera, the archetypal exile from the Soviet Empire's "totalitarian fugue," has achieved the highest degree of recognition and prominence in the West among the writers analyzed in this study. Embracing a cynical rationalism, he dethrones the lyrical posturing of revolutionary ideology while laying bare the psychopolitical foundations of totalitarianism. By deconstructing motherhood, Kundera reveals the motivation of all those ideologists who discipline and punish in the name of love. His own admiration of the West and his disgust with the East are signs of abjection and symptomatic of a literature exiled from the sphere of the once omnipotent Mother Russia. The literal crossing of the border into exile is an ambivalent act for Kundera; on the one hand, it creates an illusion of "lighter being"; on the other, it transforms the abject ties with the home country into material for literary expression. The image of the border is an existential obsession for Kundera's characters, a line of demarcation that divides and brings together, a limit that creates and destroys meaning. "It takes so little, so infinitely little, for a person to cross the border beyond which everything loses meaning: love, convictions, faith, history. Human life—and herein lies its secret—takes place in the immediate proximity of that border, even in direct contact with it; it is not miles away, but a fraction of an inch."[5]

Moving beyond the specific case of the "Other Europe," Kundera establishes the problem of the borderline as a universal determinant of the human condition in this century. The improbability of a universe of constantly shifting borders calls for the construction of an identity that can survive under conditions of perpetual crisis, an identity capable of producing meanings while resisting the forgetfulness of technological utopias. Borderline fiction, while dwelling on the specific literary, mythological, and historical codes that make up the individual identity in Slavic cultures, manifests the problem that has permeated most cultural practices beyond the "lands-in-between." The totalitarian project appears as a caricature of a more successful, although ideologically less explicit, mode of control in the West, where institutional technology, empowered by the mass consumption of ideology through products and advertising, eliminates artistic writing by demanding that literature satisfy the laws of economy.

While trying to defeat the institution by producing a version of demonic individualism, borderline fiction subjects the alien and incomprehensible world to the literary reshaping that resembles psychotic derealization. Thought is guided by the negative, parodic reading of culture, a process that demonstrates culture's mechanisms, allowing historical representations to shape and dominate the material world. This produces the discourse of the borderline, recognizable on the outside and hollow on the inside, a linguistic expression of the true-real. Kristeva sees this withdrawal into the true-real dimension of language (which prevents the Name-of-the-Father from dividing and ordering it according to the "law of death") as a way of achieving an imaginary security that avoids identifications and scorns identity. "On close inspection, all literature is probably a version of the apocalypse that seems to me rooted, no matter what its socio-historical conditions may be, on the fragile border (borderline cases) where identities (subject/object, etc.) do not exist or only barely so— double, fuzzy, heterogeneous, animal, metamorphosed, altered, abject."[6]

The rejection of both ideology and identity by the borderline writer leads to the apocalyptic assessment of a humanity whose faith in the future is opening up the path to self-destruction. Kristeva's universalist statement about "all literature" is exaggerated, especially since the doctrines of literary realism insist on mimesis, verisimilitude, and the stable identity of its protagonists. Setting itself against Lukács's ideal "fusion of the particular and the general which is the essence of realistic art," borderline fiction de-fuses the totality by foregrounding individual difference through irony and parody.[7] Just as realism appears to be a stylization of the officially enforced ideology, borderline fiction is by definition a parody of the ideologically constructed world. By insisting on the contradictions and indeterminacies inherent in the individual, solitary, alienated experience of the world, borderline writing exhibits what Kundera has called "the most grotesque version of the will to power."[8] And by attempting to impose the individual, usually poetically defamiliarized, vision of the world, the writer denies the values of the compact majority and its social norms and, flirting with graphomania, proceeds to shape a world where identities are always in question.

An inevitable question arises from the consideration of the overtly ideologized universe of communism: what are the political consequences of this type of writing practice? Will writing become an even more isolated force as it withdraws yet further into the space of subjectivity? Or will the critique of ideology from the borderline perspective of constant contradiction lead to the establishment of a political field more tolerant of difference? The violent irruption of nationalist sentiments does not seem promising in this respect. Recent political changes indicate that independent intellectuals are once again being marginalized, this time through the more effective methods of economic censorship borrowed from the West. The new nationalist elites are using the techniques of the "free market" to eliminate those works of art that do not fit their political agendas. The best-selling works are those that explore the national past and not those that in any way question the narrow and xenophobic frameworks of nationalist ideology.

The crucial role of intellectuals in the peaceful dethroning of totalitarianism in Czechoslovakia, Poland, Bulgaria, and even the Soviet Union demonstrates that writing constitutes a political force that cannot finally be restrained by the prescribed ideology. The persisting need to express subjectivity and individuality, suppressed by the monoliths of control for centuries of totalitarianism (in its feudal and Communist form), surfaces in popular political movements that promise the establishment of a community based on civic responsibilities. But, despite this hope for a liberal solution, it should be recognized that the danger of succumbing to malignant nationalism that threatens to replace the totality of communism is great. This could have devastating consequences for a culture striving to be reintegrated into the European continent from which it has been exiled through the invention of the "Iron Curtain." The rise of nationalism, evident in the entire region, paired with the revival of anti-Semitism and other forms of ethnic intolerance could push the region into yet another period of historical and cultural regression.

The tenuous situation of the borderline writer in the totalitarian sphere is already becoming a thing of the past. The improbable universe of his fiction exposed the delusions of realism (socialist and every other one), if not the assumptions of political ideology founded on "reality." The relationship between writing and power is undergoing a fundamental transformation due to the emergence of new "realities." It may turn out that the writers who fought hard to problematize the notion of "reality" constructed by totalitarian regimes have opened the doors for the emergence of cultures that may become as oppressive in due course. If there was one good thing to be retained from the "Old World," it was the belief in the possibility of understanding between nations and cultures based on common humanist values. Nationalism does not acknowledge that, but works to affirm "our" cultural identity at the expense of "their" non-culture.

Borderline fiction represents an imaginary attempt to dismantle the totality. By pointing to the imbalance in relations between the dominant institutions and marginalized individuals, this type of literature has implicitly called for the re-establishment of a balance of power, demanding that institutions be responsive to individuals. The election of a dissident playwright, Václav Havel, as president of Czechoslovakia demonstrates the political influence of intellectuals who manage to maintain their artistic integrity in the face of power. I hope that Slavic cultures will break with the simplistic dualism noted by Lotman and found a culture based on plurality and difference. At the same time I fear that this may not be enough in unmasking the phantoms of nationalism and religious fundamentalism, the forces well organized to cause a regression to an older form of totality.

Notes

introduction

1. See epigram to the work: "In the beginning, there was no earth and no people. Everywhere was the water. There were only the Lord and the devil, who at that time lived together," as quoted in Dragomanov, *Zabeležki verhu slavyanskite religiozno-etičeski legendi,* Vol. VIII of *Sbornik za narodni umotvoreniya, nauka i knižnina.* Sofia: n. p., 1892. This quote contains the germinal cultural articulation of the borderline potential within the Slavic identity. "The Lord and the devil," floating on top of the water of the maternal abyss that threatens to swallow the difference and erase the border between two separate identities, between good and evil, between light and dark, between any other opposition created by the introduction of writing.

2. I will concentrate on the Slavic cultures in Russia, Eastern and Central Europe, omitting the Germanic, Hungarian, Romanian, Albanian, Jewish, Gypsy, and other non-Slavic traditions of this culturally heterogeneous region. This omission is determined by the disciplinary boundary of this study, which belongs to the area of comparative Slavic studies.

3. I understand psychopolitics as an intersection of different historical and ideological discourses within the realm of a particular ideological, literary, or psychic space. Since ideology usually operates as an unconscious cultural construct within a particular culture, my account of Slavic literatures

may be considered simultaneously as an objective study of Slavic cultures from an external point of view and as a subjective process of self-discovery from the internal point of view, characteristic for, to use Yuri Lotman's phrase, the "bearer of culture." This inner point of view enables one to examine those semiotic traces that are inscribed on the level of the ultimate linguistic invariants of Roman Jakobson or the semiotic chora of Julia Kristeva. The inner perspective requires the study of culture as a repository of semiotic traces that are ordered by the bioenergetic charges of the organism, the famous *Trieben* of Freudian psychoanalysis. Kristeva observes the regulation that the drives exercise on the formation of meanings: "Drives involve pre-Oedipal semiotic functions and energy discharges that connect and orient the body to the mother. We must emphasize that 'drives' are always already ambiguous, simultaneously assimilating and destructive; this dualism, which has been represented as a tetrad or as a double helix, as in the configuration of the DNA or RNA molecule, makes the semiotized body a place of permanent schism." (Julia Kristeva, *Revolution in Poetic Language*, trans. Leon S. Roudiez [New York: Columbia University Press, 1984], 29.) These traces in language, which order the distribution of bioenergetic charges of the organism, are inscribed both in literature and in the body of the writer/reader of a particular culture, in this case Slavic culture. In the most archaic articulation of proto-Slavic culture, this "dualism of the drives" and their "permanent schism" are given cultural and mythological expression in the worship of the White God and the Black God (Byelobog and Chernobog). This dualism is later reinscribed within Christianity as the conflict between God and the devil, who are absolutely opposed and who regulate two different cultural zones ("high" vs. "low" culture). Politics regulates meanings through ideology, creating zones of cultural resistance that are engendered in the borderline psychic space, characteristic of Slavic culture.

4. Robin Okey, *Eastern Europe, 1740–1980* (Minneapolis: University of Minnesota Press, 1982), explains the economic origins of the so-called "XVI century turning point" that was to divide Europe into its Eastern and Western halves. "Already in the late Middle Ages, Western Europe was witnessing a slackening of the ties of the old feudal order. . . . For a while it seemed that Eastern Europe might follow a parallel course. . . . But there was to be no flowering. Feudal forces were strong enough to reverse the trend. . . . Secure in their feudal diets, the nobles in province after province from the late fifteenth century began to pour out edicts restricting free peasant movement and tightening up half-forgotten labour regulations" (17–19). This political and economic situation enabled the nobleman and the church to enforce more control over the cultural sphere, using it as the ideological

tool for the control of their subjects. While the West developed the bourgeois concept of "autonomous" culture, the East stayed locked within the
basically medieval cultural sphere.

5. Ju. M. Lotman and B. A. Uspenski, "The Role of the Dual Models in
the Dynamics of Russian Culture," in *The Semiotics of Russian Culture,*
trans. Ann Shukman, Michigan Slavic Contributions, No. 11 (Ann Arbor:
n.p., 1984).

6. The Bogumils represent the most interesting cultural phenomenon
since their rebellion is evident on a religious plane. Bogumils worshiped the
darker, female side of the Christian God, which the official church fathers
could not tolerate. It is not surprising that the Bogumils' main teaching was
gnosis, the knowledge of spirituality that stems from the observation of the
life and death process in nature, or pantheism, which twisted the Biblical
story, defamiliarized it, turned it into a dualistic, hybrid religious practice
whose dark element obviously survives in the *Ancient Bulgarian Apocryphal
Genesis* as the unconscious semiotic element (see the epigram and note 1).
Mikhail Bakhtin's demand for the study of literature as a part of an "epoch's
entire culture," but without forgetting that "the work cannot live in future
centuries without having somehow absorbed past centuries as well" results
in his theory about the memory of the genre. The materialist semiotics cannot build its knowledge solely on the foundations of the class struggle, but
has to study ways in which it articulates itself, in both its literary and speech
genres. (See M. M. Bakhtin, *Speech Genres and Other Late Essays,* trans. Vern
W. McGee [Austin: University of Texas Press, 1986], 4–6). The realm of
signification is divided into the two main hierarchical zones: a) priesthood
and nobility—high literate culture; and b) peasantry—low oral culture. The
former is ruled by the laws of the signifier and of its Christian dogma, associated with the order of high medieval iconic culture. The latter relates to the
signifier as the unconscious, oral element, whose development depends on
the spoken word, on the song, or on the ancient pagan ritual (e.g., *dodole*
rain dance in the Balkans). This repressed cultural element erupts later in
the works of Russian futurists, contextualized as the avant-garde poetry of
the new revolutionary age, and also in the borderline poetics of the post-
revolutionary Slavic fiction that sets itself against the high "revolutionary"
ideals of socialist realist literature.

7. For a detailed discussion of the origins of Byelobog and Chernobog see
Myroslava Znayenko, *The Gods of the Ancient Slavs* (Columbus: Slavica
Publishers, Inc., 1980). Znayenko gives a survey of primary sources that
mention the two opposed gods, from Helmhold's *Chronica Slavorum* to
Tatiščev's *Istorija rossiskaja* and the *Leksikon.* Also, a work by a Serbian

scholar Veselin Čajkanović, *Mit i religija u Srba* (Beograd: SKZ, 1973), concludes that a White and a Black God were common to all the Slavs. The
question posed by Dragomanov (see note 1) about the originality of the
dualistic belief in Slavic cosmogony is irrelevant here; whether it is of Assiro-
Babylonian or directly Slavic origin, the belief in dual creation is opposed to
the Judeo-Christian, monolithic story found in the Book of Genesis.

8. "Slavonic Mythology," *New Larousse Encyclopedia of Mythology*
(London: Hamlyn, 1977), 287. The connection of the feminine power with
the element of earth is very strong in all Slavic cultures. One of the chants
that the Russian peasant performs while turning to the West (the realm of
the dark god or the devil) goes like this: "Moist Mother Earth, engulf the
unclean power in thy boiling pits, in thy burning fires." This "unclean
power" shows the ambivalent presence of abjection: women are subjected to
confinement and isolation during the course of Christian history because
they are perceived as the source of the threatening, demonic power that
escapes symbolization and can therefore cause harm to the linear order of
the dominant symbolic order. See Julia Kristeva, *Powers of Horror, An Essay
on Abjection* (New York: Columbia University Press, 1984).

9. Lotman and Uspenski, *Semiotics of Russian Culture,* 6, offer an account
of the way in which high-low or top-bottom distinctions were applied to the
spatial organization of Vladimir's kingdom during the period of Christian
conquest: "The idol of Pyerun was thrown down from Kiev hills to Podol,
i.e., to where the Christian church of St. Elijah (Pyerun's Christian counterpart) stood, and the Christian church was built up above where there had
previously been a heathen temple."

10. M. E. Šermeteva, *Svad 'ba v Gamajunščine, kalužskogo uezda* (Kaluga:
n.p., 1928), 109.

11. Lotman and Uspenski, 4.

12. Peter Bürger, *Theory of the Avant-Garde* (Minneapolis: University of
Minnesota Press, 1984), 35–54.

13. Lotman and Uspenski, 5. Lotman's theory of the semiotic development of Russian culture is similar to Nietzsche's concept of the historical
return of the same element. Both Nietzsche and Lotman sense the presence
of the pagan, cyclical, and despotic mode that gradually returns under the
literate surface of Christianity. The only difference is the role of the dual
model, as opposed to the explicitly circular motion of the same, in
Nietzsche's case, superhuman element.

14. Lotman and Uspenski, 21.

15. Milivoj Nenin, "Prostori vedrine u narodnoj erotskoj poeziji,"

Gradina 9–10 (1987): 167–71. For more scatological and erotic challenges to the dominant values in Balkan societies see Daniel Weissbort's and my translation of *Crven Ban* (*Red Knight*, London: King's College, 1992).

16. This is a quote from a satirical epistle written by Kajetan Kožmian and directed against the romantic poet F. Morawski. From Dmitrij Čiževskij, *The Comparative History of Slavic Literatures* (Nashville: Vanderbilt University Press, 1971), 136.

17. Nikolai Berdyaev, *The End of Our Time* (London: Sheed & Ward, 1935), 206.

18. From the preface to Velimir Khlebnikov, *Sobranie Sochinenij* (Moscow, 1927–33).

19. From "Napoleon and I" in *Electric Iron,* Jack Hirschman and Victor Erlich, trans. (Berkeley: Maya, 1971), 46.

20. A. Ždanov, Speech on the First Congress of the Union of Soviet Writers (Moscow, 1934).

21. See Mikhail Bakhtin, *Voprosy literatury i estetiki* (Moscow: Khudožestvennaya Literatura, 1975); or in the English translation, see Mikhail Bakthin, *The Dialogic Imagination,* trans. C. Emerson and M. Holquist (Austin: University of Texas Press, 1981), 3–41.

22. For an excellent discussion of the development of socialist realism see Geofrey Hosking, *Beyond Socialist Realism* (New York: Holmes & Meier, 1980); also A. Ovcharenko, *Novye geroi—novye puti: ot M. Gor'kogo do V. Šukšina* (Moscow: Sovremennik, 1977).

23. Georg Lukács, *Realism in Our Time,* trans. John and Necke Mander (New York: Harper and Row, 1964), 97.

24. Adolf Hitler, Speech inaugurating the Great Exhibition of German Art, Munich, 1937. Quoted from Herschel B. Chipp, *Theories of Modern Art* (Berkeley: University of California Press, 1968), 480.

25. I have borrowed the concept of the Real (*Réel*) from the French psychoanalyst Jacques Lacan, *Ecrits, A Selection,* trans. Alan Sheridan (Norton & Company: New York, 1977). The Real stands "for what is neither symbolic nor imaginary, and remains foreclosed from the analytic experience, which is an experience of speech." The writer of the borderline tradition is also aware of the fact that no method of achieving the verisimilar effect of literature can circumvent the experience of speech and language. Since the Real is always refracted through the prism of the imaginary (the phantasmic register of perception) or through the symbolic (the realm of the linguistic signifier), every "reality" produced by fiction is necessarily foreclosed from the Real. That is why the borderline writer gives up the pretension of

verisimilitude and works by distorting the linear and dogmatic presentations of politically designed "reality," hoping to approach the Real by the paradoxical process of double negation.

26. See Richard Restak, *The Self Seekers* (New York: Doubleday, 1982), 147–74; James F. Masterson, *The Search for the Real Self* (New York: The Free Press, 1988), 75–107; W. W. Meissner, *Treatment of Patients in the Borderline Spectrum* (London: Jason Aronson, 1988), 3–62.

27. It is symptomatic that the Soviet soldiers who participated in the occupation of Czechoslovakia in 1968 told the citizens of Prague they came to liberate them because they loved them.

28. Milan Kundera, "A Kidnapped West or Culture Bows Out," *Granta* 11 (1984): 102.

29. "The holy fool's behavior is thoroughly imbued with didactic content. Having personal connections with the Lord, he was, as it were, surrounded by a sacred micro-space, a sort of placenta of holiness; hence behavior becomes possible which from the external point of view seems to be blasphemous, but is not so in essence. . . . It is this inner holiness that creates the conditions for the antithetically opposed exterior perception: the fact that he is encapsulated in a sacred micro-space endows his behavior with inverted character for the outside observer who is located in the world of sin. In other words, the holy fool is in effect forced to behave in an inverted way, his behavior is didactically contrasted with the qualities of this world. The attributes of anti-behavior are switched in this process from the actor to the spectators: the holy fool's behavior converts play into reality, demonstrating the unreal, deceptive nature of the external environment." In Ju. M. Lotman and B. A. Uspenskij, "New Aspects in the Study of Early Russian Culture," in *The Semiotics of Russian Culture,* trans. Ann Shukman, Michigan Slavic Contributions, No. 11 (Ann Arbor: n.p., 1984), 36–37.

30. Milan Kundera, *The Art of the Novel,* trans. Linda Asher (New York: Grove Press, 1988), 116.

31. Gilles Deleuze and Felix Guattari, *Kafka: Toward a Minor Literature,* trans. Dana Polan (Minneapolis: University of Minnesota Press, 1986), 17.

32. Deleuze and Guattari, *Kafka,* 18.

33. Witold Gombrowicz, *Ferdydurke,* trans. Eric Mosbacher (New York: Penguin, 1986), 283.

34. Gombrowicz, *Ferdydurke,* 283.

35. Gombrowicz, *Ferdydurke,* 282.

36. Gombrowicz, *Ferdydurke,* 282

37. As quoted in Kundera, *The Art of the Novel,* 138.

mikhail bulgakov

1. Rita Giuliani, "Žanrovi ruskog pučkog teatra i Majstor i Margarita M.A. Bulgakova," in *Pojmovnik ruske avangarde,* ed. Aleksandar Flaker and Dubravka Ugrešić, III (Zagreb: Grafički Zavod Hrvatske, 1985), 249–73.

2. Bulgakov's case is not exceptional in this respect. During the first years of Soviet rule, the tendency to use models from popular culture reached its culmination. The most important theatre directors of that era used the techniques borrowed from circus, from commedia dell'arte, from *balagan* (another Russian popular carnevalesque form), etc. Using these techniques, Tairov directed *Princessa Brambilla* (1920) i *Žiroflja-Žirofl'* (1922), Vahtangov adapted *Turandot* (1922), and Meyerhold directed *Smert' Tarelkina* (1922). For more information on the influence of popular theatrical forms see D. Zolotnickij, *Zori teatral'nogo Oktyabrya* (Leningrad, 1976) and S. Radlov, *Desjat' let v teatre* (Leningrad, 1929).

3. All quotes in English are from Michael Glenny's translation of the novel, M. Bulgakov, *The Master and Margarita* (New York: New American Library, 1985), hereafter referred to as *MM*.

4. Andrew Barratt, *Between Two Worlds: A Critical Introduction to "The Master and Margarita"* (Oxford: Clarendon Press, 1987), gives three examples of those "romantic" views of the Master (246-50). All three types of romantic reading tend to idealize the Master as either the "persecuted genius," as the manifestation of "romantic dissatisfaction," or as the "vessel of superior knowledge." All three of those views yield to the mythological subtext disguised under the Master's parodic appearance.

5. Linda Hutcheon, *A Poetics of Postmodernism* (New York: Routledge, 1988), 224. "The paradoxes of postmodernism work to instruct us in the inadequacies of totalizing systems and of fixed institutionalized boundaries (epistemological and ontological). Historiographic metafiction's parody and self-reflexivity function both as markers of the literary and as challenges to its limitations. Its contradictory 'contamination' of the self-consciously literary with the verifiably historical and referential challenges the borders we accept as existing between literature and the extra-literary narrative discourses which surround it: history, biography, autobiography."

Brian McHale in his book *Postmodernist Fiction* (New York: Methuen, 1987) uses Bulgakov's *The Master and Margarita* as an example of the post-modernist novel because of the carnivalesque dimension that "is subversive of monological authority" (171–72).

6. A. Ždanov, Speech on the First Congress of the Union of Soviet Writers (Moscow, 1934).

7. Vladeta Jerotić, "Gnosticizam i naše vreme," *Književna reč*, no. 325–26 (1988): 34.

8. Jerotić, "Gnosticizam . . ."

9. Kurt Rudolph, *Gnosis: The Nature and History of an Ancient Religion*, trans. Robert McLachlan Wilson (Edinburgh: T. & T. Clark Limited, 1983), 171.

10. I. Mirimsky, "Sotsial'naya fantastika Gofmana," *Literarnaya uchoba*, no. 5 (1938): 63–87.

11. M. Gorky, *O literature—stat'i i reči* (Moscow, 1937), was the first Soviet writer who attempted to re-evaluate romanticism and show that it could be useful in the new socialist society. In order to do that, he had to distinguish between the "passive" romanticism that is characterized by "a sterile absorption in the inner world" while trying to solve the "fateful riddles of life and death," and the "active" kind that "strives to strengthen man's will to live and provoke in him rebelliousness towards reality and against every oppression." This second version is obviously the basis for Ždanov's concept of the "revolutionary romanticism," an essential spice for successful socialist realist literature (see Introduction, 22).

12. Rudolph, *Gnosis*, 144.

13. "The Bogomilian writings in Old Church Slavonic still enjoyed throughout the Middle Ages great popularity and strongly influenced the Old Slavonic popular literature. The songs of the beggars at the doors of Russian churches still preserved Bogomilian thought patterns." Rudolph, *Gnosis*, 375.

14. Jerotić, "Gnosticizam . . ."

15. Rudolph, *Gnosis*, 76.

16. Quoted in Elaine Pagels, *The Gnostic Gospels* (New York: Random House, 1981), 66.

witold gombrowicz

1. Witold Gombrowicz, *Diary*, vol. 1, trans. Lillian Vallee (Evanston: Northwestern University Press, 1988), 77.

2. All quotations from the novel are unfortunately from Eric Mosbacher's problematic translation of *Ferdydurke* (Penguin: New York, 1986), hereafter referred to as *F.* The original edition of *Ferdydurke* (Warsaw: Rój, 1937) contains a host of neologisms and word games that have been left out in Mosbacher's translation. Ewa Thompson, *Witold Gombrowicz* (Boston: Twayne Publishers, 1979), remarks on some difficulties of Gombrowicz's literary idiom. "Thus accordingly, they [Gombrowicz's word games] have often been eliminated from the translations of his works. However, anyone familiar with Polish readily notices that in spite of the anomalous nature of many of Gombrowicz's words and rhythms, they sound strangely familiar nonetheless. In some cases, Gombrowicz's Polish seems rough, even startling at first, but this reaction is soon replaced by a realization that there is in the works the same joyful celebration of language which can be found in the poems of the futurists written at the beginning of this century. Gombrowicz brings forth the latent structures of language, and activates potentialities of it that have long been lying fallow. His usages—and with them, bits and pieces of his world view—are presently accommodating themselves to a place in contemporary colloquial Polish" (111). Gombrowicz is the most radical of the borderline novelists in this respect: he carries out Kristeva's "revolution in poetic language" not only on the level of the novelistic genre, but also on the level of the literary style, which is marked by the anarchic desire to explode the conventions of the existing canon.

3. Gombrowicz, *Diary,* 79.

4. Peter Sloterdijk, *Critique of Cynical Reason,* trans. Michael Eldred (Minneapolis: University of Minnesota Press, 1987), 245.

5. Sloterdijk uses the Diogenes figure in his *Critique of Cynical Reason* as a prototype of a postmodern intellectual who problematizes every form of ideology in order to affirm the kynical relativity of existence: "As anti-theoretician, anti-dogmatist, anti-scholar, he emits an impulse that resounds everywhere where thinkers strive for a 'knowledge for free people,' free also from the strictures of a school, and with this he begins a series in which names like Montaigne, Voltaire, Nietzsche, Feyerabend, and others appear. It is a line of philosophizing that suspends the *esprit de sérieux.*" (160). One could easily add Gombrowicz's name to the list of Sloterdijk's "kynical" thinkers, who use irony and parody to reveal the simultaneous truth and falsity of their experience of the world.

6. Gombrowicz, *Diary,* 130. Youth and adolescence are the themes that have established Gombrowicz in the history of Polish literature. Czeslaw Milosz, in his *History of Polish Literature* (Berkeley: University of California Press, 1983), summarizes Gombrowicz's obsession with this theme: "An

adolescent is a set of contradictions which may be envisaged as possibilities; he can take one or another form. When he is caught in the world of adults, he assumes a form not his own but pre-existing, elaborated through mutual relationships between adults" (432–33). What Milosz overlooks is "the influence of war" that causes the resurgence of "regressive powers" conducive to the glorification of youth. Once more, the historical powers are at work, forcing the identity to take a certain ideological form. Gombrowicz expects youth to be his "haven from 'values' and culture," a non-conflictual existence that is impossible in the ideologized universe of wartime Europe.

7. Gombrowicz, *Diary*, 132.

8. Gombrowicz, *Diary*, 132.

9. Gombrowicz, *Diary*, 132.

10. Milosz in his *History of Polish Literature* remarks that Gombrowicz's method consists exactly in "a game of constant provocation, cornering the reader into an admission of unpalatable truths" (432). Gombrowicz transforms himself into a parodic literary dictator who forces readers to embrace his version of the world, rather than trying to please the so-called average reader. This is probably the cause of his relatively small commercial success.

11. The return of the pagan element is evident in Gombrowicz's use of the literary language. "Gombrowicz mocks the gentility of Polish literary language. He ridicules the superficial smoothness of style by which some writers contemporary to him gained the reputation of great stylists. He makes the aristocratic characters in his works use peasant dialects and city jargon." Ewa Thompson, *Witold Gombrowicz*, 107. This type of parodic defamiliarization points to the double-bind nature of Polish cultural identity, a fact that the aristocracy and the cultural elite ignore or disguise by masking themselves as "proper Europeans."

12. Gombrowicz, *Diary*, 136.

13. Gombrowicz, *Diary*, 145.

14. Gombrowicz, *Diary*, 116.

15. Gombrowicz, *Diary*, 116.

16. Gombrowicz, *Diary*, 116.

17. Gombrowicz, *Diary*, 117.

18. Gombrowicz, *Diary*, 116–17.

19. Gombrowicz, *Diary*, 117.

20. Gombrowicz, *Diary*, 118.

21. Gombrowicz, *Diary*, 118–19.

22. Gombrowicz, *Diary*, 145.

23. Ewa Thompson, *Witold Gombrowicz*, 106, notes the author's scorn for

both realistic and romantic literature, while going back to the eighteenth-
century novelistic articulations of rationalism: "Gombrowicz believed that
the roots of good Polish prose go back to the seventeenth and eighteenth
century, which in Poland meant baroque and late baroque. The literature of
that period was still free of *Weltschmertz* and self-consciousness; it was joyful
and unhampered by rules of propriety or fashion." In addition, this literature still believed in the power of thought, in both its critical and parodic
articulations.

24. Gombrowicz, *Diary*, 144.
25. Gombrowicz, *Diary*, 118.
26. Gombrowicz, *Diary*, 118.

danilo kiš

1. Danilo Kiš, *Grobnica za Borisa Davidoviča* (Beograd: BIGZ, 1980).
The citations in English are from Danilo Kiš, *A Tomb for Boris Davidovich*,
trans. Duška Mikić-Mitchell (New York: Harcourt Brace Jovanovich, 1978),
hereafter referred to as *TBD*.

2. Danilo Kiš, *Čas Anatomije* (Beograd: Nolit, 1981), 54.

3. In a conversation with Philip Roth, Kundera gives a definition of the
novel as a borderline genre par excellence, echoing Bakhtin's conceptions of
the polyphonic character of the genre: "A novel is a long piece of synthetic
prose based on play with invented characters. These are the only limits. By
the term synthetic I have in mind the novelist's desire to grasp his subject
from all sides and in the fullest possible completeness. Ironic essay, novelistic
narrative, autobiographical essay, historic fact, flight of fantasy: The synthetic power of the novel is capable of combining everything into a unified
whole like the voices of polyphonic music. The unity of a book need not
stem from the plot, but can be provided by the theme." From Milan
Kundera, *The Book of Laughter and Forgetting*, trans. Michael Henry Heim
(New York: Penguin, 1981), 323.

4. To emphasize the literary quality of Fedukin's prose, Kiš talks about his
descriptions of nature, no doubt with tongue in cheek, ironically equating
literary realism with the cruelty of the police investigator: "the austere
beauty of the Siberian landscape, the sunrise over the frozen tundra, diluvial
rains and treacherous waters cutting through the taiga, the silence of distant
lakes, their steel color—all of which testifies to his undeniable literary
talent."

5. See Gilles Deleuze and Félix Guattari, *Kafka: Toward a Minor Literature,* trans. Dana Polan (Minneapolis: University of Minnesota Press, 1986).

6. Milan Kundera, *The Art of the Novel,* trans. Linda Asher (New York: Grove Press, 1988), 116.

7. Danilo Kiš, "Izvod iz knjige živih," *NIN,* 22 Oct. 1989, 38–39.

8. Kiš, "Izvod . . . ," 39.

9. Danilo Kiš, "Istinitost fiktivne tvorevine," *NIN,* 22 Oct. 1989, 38.

10. According to Šklovsky, "the literature of the fact" is a search for identity of the individual personality in the chaotic flow of factual events. "Life evolves through fragments which belong to different structures. The unconnected moments of one's life are united only through one's exterior, through non-body" (*Sentimental'noe putešestvie,* 1923). Hans Günther, "Literatura fakta," *Pojmovnik ruske avangarde,* No. 1 (1984), 65.

milan kundera

1. In a recent interview (Ian McEwan, "An Interview with Milan Kundera," *Granta,* No. 11 [1984]: 23) Kundera makes a remark that supports this hypothesis. After explaining how his books were banned in Czechoslovakia after the Russian invasion, he comments on writing within the Western context: "Your immediate public has its demands, its tastes; it exerts an influence on you without your being aware of it." I would like to examine the interplay between Kundera's poetics of criticism and the demand from his imagined public that influences him while "he is not aware of it."

2. Julia Kristeva develops the theory of abjection in her book *Powers of Horror* (Julia Kristeva, *Powers of Horror* [New York: Columbia University Press, 1982]). Abjection is the pre-Oedipal horror of being that can never be fully symbolized, although it underlies all signification. Its source is the power of maternal protection which keeps the pre-Oedipal subject bound to her passivity. Writing is one of the ways by which the subject is resurrected from abjection: the ability to reject, divide, and repeat through naming helps the subject to imagine the abject and displace it through language. Corruption is the moral expression of abjection, racism its social dimension, and misogyny its gender component. Kundera's destiny of exile bears the mark of abjection: he wishes to reject his "Eastern" past and achieve a proper "Western" identity, to denounce the abject ideology of communism and embrace the signs of patriarchal culture.

3. Following Kristeva's argument about the nature of chora as the irreducible nonverbal element of language, I believe in the material organization of being and its meanings grounded in the diachronic structures of one's native tongue. (See Julia Kristeva, *Revolution in Poetic Language* [New York: Columbia University Press, 1984]). The articulation of drives in the thetic phase depends on the linguistic structures that differ from language to language. So an ontolinguistic determination is a specific mode of being that is developed, distilled, and deposited within the structures of one's native tongue. The occurrence of "untranslatable" words within a structure of a particular language make this hypothesis possible: *saudade* in Portuguese and *litost* in Czech are two prominent examples. These words express a mode of being that is fully experienced only by the native speaker, demonstrating that being can be inscribed in language and experienced between those who practice it.

4. Milan Kundera, *Life Is Elsewhere,* trans. Peter Kussi (New York: Viking Penguin, 1986), hereafter referred to as *LIE.* The titles of the chapters tell a story of their own; those dealing with "the Poet" are devoted to "important" moments in his life: birth, masturbation, running away, jealousy, and death. The parody of "poetic" destiny is complemented by two other chapters that show "the Poet's" ego ideal ("Xavier") and Kundera's ideal of hedonism ("The Middle-Aged Man").

5. The photograph is removed again after a few years, when the mother finds out that the father was cheating on her with a Jewish girl. He was caught in the ghetto by the Nazis—this adultery was the real reason for his arrest and execution. Is it possible that the father embodies the true spirit of lyricism? Isn't he ready to die for love?

6. We have to remind ourselves of the fact that the poet is not yet born. All of these elaborations are preparing his place in the world, which Kundera, like Lacan and Borges, sees as an interplay of symbolic differences. Whether it is the Symbolic Order or the Library of Babel, the subject has to yield to its pre-existing structures and insert itself into it. Jaromil is a Platonic copy of Apollo, a constant fading of the idea of beauty that leads to his grotesque form.

7. Following Melanie Klein's teaching, Kristeva treats the formation of this specular, pre-Oedipal personality structure as the reflection of the maternal phallus. The law of maternal desire is guided by this impossible object, by the phantasm that never finds a support in the True-Real, and therefore necessarily causes the ambivalence of abjection. It turns out that Jaromil's destiny is exactly that—a reflection of Maman's desire, which leads Jaromil into dependence, moral corruption, and death.

8. At this moment, Kundera returns to the Real by double negation. If Jaromil can be his own critic, so can his creator. Kundera reveals the method of his poetics of criticism: he takes a naive and foolish poet like Jaromil and patiently exposes his formative mechanisms. But this method reveals the Real structure underlying his method: the author is rewriting and laughing at his own idealistic youth—Jaromil's poetry and his essays about it converge and expose Kundera's artistic device.

9. I have always found the designation of "internal exile" highly significant. While still attached to the body of Mother Russia, the dissident is forced to look for signs of abjection "inside." This condition of "internal exile" seems to slowly prevail among the intellectuals not only in socialism, but even in the larger context. Thinking itself becomes a form of dissidence in a world whose ideals are control and power.

10. Milan Kundera, "A Kidnapped West or Culture Bows Out," *Granta*, no. 11 (1984): 100.

11. It is difficult not to make this parallel: both Kundera and Kristeva are exiles; they have both attempted to sever the ties of abjection that bind their native Czechoslovakia and Bulgaria to the body of Mother Russia. Also, their distant position enables them to recognize the nature of the tie, the monolithic ideology that does not tolerate difference.

12. Kundera, "The Kidnapped West," 104

13. A notable exception is Tamina from *The Book of Laughter and Forgetting* whose melancholy and silence are distinctively Slavic. Why does Kundera repress and reject his cultural heritage? Isn't the Moravian mission that came from the Byzantine "obscure depths" responsible for Czech literacy and literature that he tries to preserve with such passion? Why does he try to prove his "Westernness" and reject his "Slavic soul"? The Slavic heritage is the abject element Kundera wants removed from his writing by the surgical technique of his critical style.

the rise of the nation

1. Franz Kafka, "The Great Wall and the Tower of Babel," in *Basic Kafka* (New York: Washington Square Press, 1979), 168.

2. Julia Kristeva, "A New Type of Intellectual: The Dissident," trans. Seán Hand, in *Kristeva Reader*, ed. Toril Moi (New York: Columbia University Press, 1986), 299.

3. Kristeva, "A New Type . . . ," 296.

4. Milan Kundera, *The Art of the Novel,* trans. Linda Asher (New York: Grove Press, 1986), 139.

5. Milan Kundera, *The Book of Laughter and Forgetting,* trans. Michael Henry Heim (New York: Knopf, 1980), 206–07.

6. Julia Kristeva, *Powers of Horror,* trans. Leon S. Roudiez (New York, Columbia University Press), 207.

7. Georg Lukács, *Realism in Our Time,* trans. John and Necke Mander (New York: Harper & Row, 1964), 45.

8. Milan Kundera, *The Art of the Novel,* trans. Linda Asher (New York: Grove Press, 1988), 131.

References

Alexinsky, G. "Slavonic Mythology." *New Larousse Encyclopedia of Mythology.* 1977 edition.

Bakhtin, M. M. *The Dialogic Imagination.* Translated by C. Emerson and M. Holquist. Austin: University of Texas Press, 1981.

——————. *Speech Genres and Other Late Essays.* Translated by Vern W. McGee. Austin: University of Texas Press, 1986.

——————. *Voprosy literatury i estetiki.* Moscow: Khudožestvennaya Literatura, 1981.

Barratt, Andrew. *Between Two Worlds: A Critical Introduction to The Master and Margarita.* Oxford: Clarendon Press, 1987.

Beatie, B. A., and P. W. Powell, "Story and Symbol: Notes towards a Structural Analysis of Bulgakov's *The Master and Margarita.*" *Russian Literature Triquarterly,* 15 (1978): 219–51.

Belza, I. F. "Genealogiya *Mastera i Margarity.*" *Kontekst 1978* (Moscow, 1978): 156–248.

Benz, Ernst. *The Eastern Orthodox Church: Its Thought and Life.* Translated by Richard and Clara Winston. New York: Doubleday, 1963.

Berdyaev, Nikolai. *The End of Our Time.* London: Sheed & Ward, 1935.

Birnbaum, Marianne D. "History and Human Relationships in the Fiction of Danilo Kiš." *Cross Currents,* no. 8 (1989): 346–50.

Boyers, Robert. "Between East and West: A Letter to Milan Kundera." In *Atrocity and Amnesia: The Political Novel since 1945,* 212–33. Oxford: Oxford University Press, 1985.

188 ────────. "Gombrowicz and *Ferdydurke*: The Tyranny of Form," *Centennial Review*, no. 14 (1970): 284–312.

Brand, Glenn. "Kundera and the Dialectic of Repetition." *Cross Currents*, no. 6 (1987): 461–72.

Bulgakov, Mikhail. *The Master and Margarita*. Translated by Michael Glenny. New York: New American Library, 1985.

────────. *Master i Margarita*. Moscow: Romany, 1973.

Bürger, Peter. *Theory of the Avant-Garde*. Translated by Michael Shaw. Minneapolis: University of Minnesota Press, 1984.

Chipp, B. *Theories of Modern Art*. Berkley: University of California Press, 1968.

Čajkanović, Veselin. *Mit i religija u Srba*. Beograd: SKZ, 1973.

────────. *O magiji i religiji*. Beograd: Prosveta, 1985.

Čiževskij, Dmitrij. *The Comparative History of Slavic Literatures*. Nashville: Vanderbilt University Press, 1971.

Čudakova, M. O. "Tvorčeskaya istoriya romana M. Bulgakova *Master i Margarita*." *Voprosy literatury*, 1, (1976): 218–53.

Deleuze, Gilles, and Felix Guattari. *Kafka: Toward a Minor Literature*. Translated by Dana Polan. Minneapolis: University of Minnesota Press, 1986.

Demborog, Jan. "Inny Gombrowicz." Tygodnik Powszechny, 31 (1977): 3.

Dragomanov, Mikhailo Petrovič. *Zabeležki verhu slavyanskite religiozno-etičeski legendi*. Vol VIII of *Sbornik za narodni umotvoreniya, nauka i knižnina*. Sofia: n.p., 1892.

Eagleton, Terry. "Estrangement and Irony." *Salmagundi*, No. 73 (1987): 25–32.

Falkiewicz, Andrzej. "Symetryczna meka analogii i analogiczna meka symetrii." *Dialog*, 20 (1975): 136–52.

Flaker, Aleksander, and Dubravka Ugrešić, editors. *Pojmovnik Ruske Avangarde Vol. 3*. Zagreb: Grafički Zavod Hrvatske, 1985.

Frank, M. K. "The Mystery of the Master's Final Destination." *Canadian-American Slavic Studies*, 15 (1981): 287–94.

Freud, Sigmund. *The Standard Edition of the Complete Psychological Works*. London: The Hogarth Press, 1953.

Fuentes, Carlos. "El otro K." *Vuelta*, no. 28 (1979): 22–29.

Gasparov, B. "Iz nablydeniy nad motivnoy strukturoy romana M. A. Bulgakova *Master i Margarita*." *Slavica Hierosolymitana*, no. 3 (1978): 198–251.

Giuliani, Rita. "Žanrovi ruskog pučkog teatra i *Majstor i Margarita* M. A.

Bulgakova," in *Pojmovnik Ruske Avangarde III*. Eds. Aleksandar Flaker
and Dubravka Ugrešić. Zagreb: Grafički Zavod Hrvatske, 1985. 249–73.

Glenny, Michael. "Existential Thought in Bulgakov's *The Master and Margarita*." *Canadian-American Slavic Studies*, 15 (1981): 238–49.

Goethe, J. W. von. *Faust*. Translated by Barker Fairley. Toronto: n.p., 1970.

Gombrowicz, Witold. *Diary*. Translated by Lillian Vallee. Evanston: Northwestern University Press, 1988.

—————. *Dziennik 1957-1961*. Paris: Institut Litteraire, 1962.

—————. *Ferdydurke*. Warsaw: Roj, 1937.

—————. *Ferdydurke*. Translated by Eric Mosbacher. New York: Penguin, 1986.

Gorky, Maksim. *O literature—stat'i i reči*. Moscow: n.p., 1937.

Gus', M. "Goryat li rukopisi?" *Znamya*, 12 (1968): 213–20.

Haber, E. C. "The Mythic Structure of Bulgakov's *The Master and Margarita*." *Russian Review*, 4 (1975): 382–409.

Hamšik, Dušan. *Writers against Rulers*. Translated by D. Orpington. New York: Vintage Books, 1971.

Hosking, Geoffrey. *Beyond Socialist Realism*. New York: Homes and Meier, 1980.

Hutcheon, Linda. *The Poetics of Postmodernism*. New York: Routledge, 1988.

Ionesco, Eugene. "Dissidence, litterature et verite: A' propos de Milan Kundera." *Commantaire*, 11 (1980): 468–70.

Jakobson, Roman. *Selected Writings*. The Hague: Mouton, 1962.

Jarzebsky, Jerzy. "Anatomia Gombrowicza." *Teksty*, 1 (1972): 114–32.

Jelenski, Constantin, and Dominique de Roux, editors. *Gombrowicz*. Paris: Editions de l'Herne, 1971.

Jerotić, Vladeta. "Gnosticizam i naše vreme." *Književna reč*, no. 325–326 (1988), 34.

Jovanović, Mihajlo. "*Yevangeliye ot Matfeya* kak literaturny istočnik *Mastera i Margarity*." *Canadian-American Slavic Studies*, 15 (1981): 259–311.

Khlebnikov, Velimir. *Electric Iron*. Translated by Jack Hirschman and Victor Erlich. Berkeley: Maya, 1977.

—————. *Sobranie Sočineniy*. Moscow: n.p. , 1927–1933.

Kimball, Roger. "The Ambiguities of Milan Kundera." *New Criterion* (January 1986): 5–13.

Kiš, Danilo. *Čas anatomije*. Beograd: Nolit, 1981.

—————. *Grobnica za Borisa Davidoviča*. Beograd: BIGZ, 1980.

—————. *A Tomb for Boris Davidovich*. Translated by Duška Mikić-Mitchell. New York: Harcourt Brace Jovanovich, 1978.

Kleberg, Lars. "On the Border: Milan Kundera's *The Book of Laughter and Forgetting*." *Scando-Slavica*, 30 (1984): 57–72.

Kristeva, Julia. *Powers of Horror: An Essay on Abjection*. Translated Leon S. Roudiez. New York: Columbia University Press, 1984.

—————. *Revolution in Poetic Language*. Translated by Leon S. Roudiez. New York: Columbia University Press, 1984.

Krugovoy, G. "Gnostičesky roman M. Bulgakova." *Novy žurnal*, no. 134 (1979): 47–81.

Kundera, Milan. *The Art of the Novel*. Translated by Linda Asher. New York: Grove Press, 1988.

—————. *The Book of Laughter and Forgetting*. Translated Michael Henry Heim. New York: Knopf, 1980.

—————. "A Kidnapped West or Culture Bows Out." *Granta*, No. 11 (1984): 95–118.

—————. *Life is Elsewhere*. Translated by Peter Kussi. New York: Knopf, 1974.

Lacan, Jacques. *Ecrits: A Selection*. Translated by Alan Sheridan. New York: Norton & Company, 1977.

Lakšin, Vladimir. "Roman M. Bulgakova *Master i Margarita*." *Novy mir*, no. 6 (1968): 284–311.

LeGrand, Eva. "L'Esthetique de la variation romanesque chez Kundera." *L'Infini*, no. 5 (1984): 56–64.

Liehm, Antonin. "Milan Kundera: Czech Writer." In *Czech Literature since 1956: A Symposium*. William E. Harkins and Paul I. Trensky, editors, 40–55. New York: Bohemica, 1980.

Lotman, Yu., and B. A. Uspenski, *The Semiotics of Russian Culture*. Translated by Ann Shukman. Ann Arbor: Michigan Slavic Contributions, 1984.

Lukács, Georg. *Realism in Our Time*. Translated by John and Necke Mander. New York: Harper and Row, 1964.

Masterson, James F. *The Search for the Real Self*. New York: The Free Press, 1988.

McHale, Brian. *Postmodernist Fiction*. New York: Methuen, 1987.

Meissner, W. W. *Treatment of Patients in the Borderline Spectrum*. London: Jason Aronson, 1988.

Mencwel, Andrzej. "Antygroteska Gombrowicza." In *Z problemow literatury polskiey XX wieku*, Vol. 2, A. Brodzka and Z. Zabicki, editors. Warsaw: Panstwowy Instytut Wydawniczy, 1965.

Milosz, Czeslaw. *The History of Polish Literature*. Berkeley: University of California Press, 1983.

Mirimsky, I. "Sotsial'naya fantastika Gofmana." *Literarnaya učoba,* no. 5 (1938): 63–87.

Musial, Grzegorz. "Karafka baczewskiego." *Tworczosć,* no. 11/12 (1986), 146–57.

Nenin, Milivoj. "Prostori vedrine u narodnoj erotskoj poeziji." *Gradina,* 9–10 (1987): 167–71.

Nietzsche, Friedrich. *Basic Writings of Nietzsche.* Translated by Walter Kaufmann. New York: Modern Library, 1968.

Okey, Robin. *Eastern Europe, 1740–1980.* Minneapolis: University of Minnesota Press, 1982.

Ovčarenko, A. *Novye geroi—novye puti ot M. Gor'kogo do V. Šukšina.* Moscow: Sovremennik, 1977.

Pagels, Elaine. *The Gnostic Gospels.* New York: Random House, 1981.

Pochoda, Elizabeth. "Overlapping Delusions." Translated by Peter Kussi. *Nation,* 2 (October 1976): 311–13.

Porter, Robert. *Milan Kundera: A Voice from Central Europe.* Aarhus: Arkona Press, 1981.

Pruit, D. B., "St. John and Bulgakov: The Model of a Parody of Christ." *Canadian-American Slavic Studies,* 15 (1981): 312–20.

Radlov, S. *Desjat' let v teatre.* Leningrad: n.p., 1929.

Restak, Richard. *The Self Seekers.* New York: Doubleday, 1982.

Ricard, Francois. "Le point de vue de Satan." *Liberte,* no. 21: 58–66.

Richterova, Sylvie. "I romanzi di Kundera e i problemi della cominicazione." *Strumenti Critici* (June 1981): 308–34.

Rudolph, Kurt. *Gnosis: The Nature and History of an Ancient Religion.* Translator Robert McLachlan Wilson. Edinburgh: T & T. Clark Limited, 1983.

Sandauer, Artur. *Bez taryfy uglowej.* Cracow: Wydawnictwo Literackie, 1959.

Schultz, Bruno. "Ferdydurke," *Proza.* Cracow. Wydawnictwo Literackie, 1964, 481–91.

Segre, Cesare. "Caos e cosmo in Gombrowicz." *I segni e la critica.* Torino: Einaudi, 1969, 243–50.

Sloterdijk, Peter. *Critique of Cynical Reason.* Translated by Michael Eldred. Minneapolis: University of Minnesota Press, 1987.

Šermeteva, M. E. *Svad'ba v Gamajunščine, kalužskogo uezda.* Kaluga, n.p., 1928.

Thompson, Ewa M., *Witold Gombrowicz.* Boston: Twayne Publishers, 1979.

Volle, Jacques. *Gombrowicz: bourreau-matryr.* Paris: Christian Bourgeois, 1972.

192   Znayenko, Miroslava. *The Gods of the Ancient Slavs.* Columbus: Slavica
          Publishers, 1980.
      Zolotnickij, D. *Zori teatral'nogo Oktyabrya.* Leningrad: n.p., 1976.
      Ždanov, A. *Speech on the First Congress of the Union of Soviet Writers.*
          Moscow, 1934.

borderline culture

Index